P9-AGU-625

Strategies proven to work.

Content instruction created just for the Lower Level ISEE. Practice to reinforce learning.

- ✓ Strategies to use for each section of the Lower Level ISEE
- ✓ Content instruction specific to the test and age-appropriate
- ✓ Drills and practice sets to build skills and confidence
- ✓ Full-length practice tests to show students what to expect and avoid surprises on test day (*Success on the Lower Level ISEE* and *The Best Unofficial Practice Tests* only)

Complete selection of Lower Level ISEE titles now available from Test Prep Works LLC:

Success on the Lower Level ISEE: A Complete Course
- Strategies for each section of the test
- Reading and vocabulary drills
- In-depth math content instruction with practice sets
- 1 full-length practice test

30 Days to Acing the Lower Level ISEE
- Strategies for each section of the test
- Fifteen "workouts", each providing practice problems and detailed explanations for every section of the test
- Perfect for additional practice or homework

The Best Unofficial Practice Tests for the Lower Level ISEE
- 2 additional full-length practice tests

Test Prep Works, LLC,

PROVIDES A NEW APPROACH TO MATERIALS

Are you a professional educator?

You know your students. You know the test.

Shouldn't your materials reflect that?

The Test Prep Works advantages include:

- In-depth instruction and practice specific to the test your students are taking
- Buy only the books that you need, when you need them
- A low, one-time setup fee with no minimum purchases

TEST PREP WORKS

CAN PROVIDE MATERIALS FOR YOUR SCHOOL OR TUTORING COMPANY. WE OFFER THE ABILITY TO CUSTOMIZE OUR MATERIALS TO REFLECT THE IDENTITY OF YOUR SCHOOL OR COMPANY.

Please visit www.TestPrepWorks.com for more information

THE BEST *Unofficial* PRACTICE TESTS
FOR THE Lower Level ISEE

Christa Abbott, M.Ed.

Copyright © 2014 Test Prep Works, LLC. All rights reserved. Except as permitted under the Copyright Act of 1976, no part of this publication may be reproduced or distributed in any forms or by any means, or stored in a data base or retrieval system, without the prior written permission of the publisher.

Published by:
Test Prep Works, LLC
PO Box 100572
Arlington, VA 22210
www.TestPrepWorks.com

ISEE is a registered trademark of the ERB. They have not endorsed nor are they associated with this book.

For information about buying this title in bulk, or for editions with customized covers or content, please contact us at sales@testprepworks.com or (703) 944-6727.

Neither the author nor the publisher of this book claims responsibility for the accuracy of this book or the outcome of students who use these materials.

ISBN: 978-1-939090-11-9

Contents

How To Use This Book

The tests in this book will give you an idea of the types of questions you will see, the concepts that are being tested, and the format and timing of the Lower Level ISEE. You will also get a sense of how the scoring works – one point is given for correct answers and nothing is subtracted for incorrect answers.

Try to work through the test in "real conditions" to get a sense of what it feels like to take a test of this length, which may be longer than what you are used to. Be sure to time yourself on each section and stop when the time is up, just like you will have to on test day.

The following chart lays out the general timing of the test:

Section	Time
Verbal Reasoning – 34 questions	20 minutes
Quantitative Reasoning – 38 questions	35 minutes
--- Five-minute break ---	
Reading Comprehension – 25 questions	25 minutes
Mathematics Achievement – 30 questions	30 minutes
--- Five-minute break ---	
Essay	30 minutes

After you complete Practice Test 1, check all of your answers. Figure out WHY you missed the questions that you answered incorrectly. Then, think about what you would do differently BEFORE you start Practice Test 2.

About the Author

Christa Abbott has been a private test prep tutor for more than a decade, helping her students gain admission to some of the top independent schools in the country. She has now used that experience to develop materials that help students prepare for independent school admissions tests. The approaches used in these books are based on the latest research about how students learn, so that preparation can be an effective and efficient use of time. These materials are also written to be developmentally appropriate for the ages of the students taking the tests.

Christa is a graduate of Middlebury College and received her Masters in Education from the University of Virginia, a program nationally recognized for its excellence. She resides in Arlington, VA, with her husband and three children. Christa continues to coach students one-on-one in the Washington, D.C., area as well as students all over the world via the internet. For more information on these services, please visit www.ChristaAbbott.com.

About Test Prep Works, LLC

Test Prep Works, LLC, was founded to provide effective materials for test preparation. Its founder, Christa Abbott, spent years looking for effective materials for the private school entrance exams but came up empty-handed. The books available combined several different tests and while there are overlaps, they are not the same test. Christa found this to be overwhelming for students who were in elementary and middle school and that just didn't seem necessary. Christa developed her own materials to use with students that are specific for each level of the test and are not just adapted from other books. Now, these materials are available to the general public as well as other tutors. Please visit www.TestPrepWorks.com to view a complete array of offerings as well as sign up for a newsletter with recent news and developments in the world of admissions and test preparation.

Answer Sheets

The following pages contain answer sheets for each of the two practice tests. Additional copies can be downloaded at:

www.testprepworks.com/student/download

Practice Test 1

Section 1: Verbal Reasoning

1 (A) (B) (C) (D)	**13** (A) (B) (C) (D)	**24** (A) (B) (C) (D)
2 (A) (B) (C) (D)	**14** (A) (B) (C) (D)	**25** (A) (B) (C) (D)
3 (A) (B) (C) (D)	**15** (A) (B) (C) (D)	**26** (A) (B) (C) (D)
4 (A) (B) (C) (D)	**16** (A) (B) (C) (D)	**27** (A) (B) (C) (D)
5 (A) (B) (C) (D)	**17** (A) (B) (C) (D)	**28** (A) (B) (C) (D)
6 (A) (B) (C) (D)	**18** (A) (B) (C) (D)	**29** (A) (B) (C) (D)
7 (A) (B) (C) (D)	**19** (A) (B) (C) (D)	**30** (A) (B) (C) (D)
8 (A) (B) (C) (D)	**20** (A) (B) (C) (D)	**31** (A) (B) (C) (D)
9 (A) (B) (C) (D)	**21** (A) (B) (C) (D)	**32** (A) (B) (C) (D)
10 (A) (B) (C) (D)	**22** (A) (B) (C) (D)	**33** (A) (B) (C) (D)
11 (A) (B) (C) (D)	**23** (A) (B) (C) (D)	**34** (A) (B) (C) (D)
12 (A) (B) (C) (D)		

Section 2: Quantitative Reasoning

1 (A) (B) (C) (D)	**14** (A) (B) (C) (D)	**27** (A) (B) (C) (D)
2 (A) (B) (C) (D)	**15** (A) (B) (C) (D)	**28** (A) (B) (C) (D)
3 (A) (B) (C) (D)	**16** (A) (B) (C) (D)	**29** (A) (B) (C) (D)
4 (A) (B) (C) (D)	**17** (A) (B) (C) (D)	**30** (A) (B) (C) (D)
5 (A) (B) (C) (D)	**18** (A) (B) (C) (D)	**31** (A) (B) (C) (D)
6 (A) (B) (C) (D)	**19** (A) (B) (C) (D)	**32** (A) (B) (C) (D)
7 (A) (B) (C) (D)	**20** (A) (B) (C) (D)	**33** (A) (B) (C) (D)
8 (A) (B) (C) (D)	**21** (A) (B) (C) (D)	**34** (A) (B) (C) (D)
9 (A) (B) (C) (D)	**22** (A) (B) (C) (D)	**35** (A) (B) (C) (D)
10 (A) (B) (C) (D)	**23** (A) (B) (C) (D)	**36** (A) (B) (C) (D)
11 (A) (B) (C) (D)	**24** (A) (B) (C) (D)	**37** (A) (B) (C) (D)
12 (A) (B) (C) (D)	**25** (A) (B) (C) (D)	**38** (A) (B) (C) (D)
13 (A) (B) (C) (D)	**26** (A) (B) (C) (D)	

Section 3: Reading Comprehension

1 (A) (B) (C) (D)	**10** (A) (B) (C) (D)	**18** (A) (B) (C) (D)
2 (A) (B) (C) (D)	**11** (A) (B) (C) (D)	**19** (A) (B) (C) (D)
3 (A) (B) (C) (D)	**12** (A) (B) (C) (D)	**20** (A) (B) (C) (D)
4 (A) (B) (C) (D)	**13** (A) (B) (C) (D)	**21** (A) (B) (C) (D)
5 (A) (B) (C) (D)	**14** (A) (B) (C) (D)	**22** (A) (B) (C) (D)
6 (A) (B) (C) (D)	**15** (A) (B) (C) (D)	**23** (A) (B) (C) (D)
7 (A) (B) (C) (D)	**16** (A) (B) (C) (D)	**24** (A) (B) (C) (D)
8 (A) (B) (C) (D)	**17** (A) (B) (C) (D)	**25** (A) (B) (C) (D)
9 (A) (B) (C) (D)		

Section 4: Mathematics Achievement

1 (A) (B) (C) (D)	**11** (A) (B) (C) (D)	**21** (A) (B) (C) (D)
2 (A) (B) (C) (D)	**12** (A) (B) (C) (D)	**22** (A) (B) (C) (D)
3 (A) (B) (C) (D)	**13** (A) (B) (C) (D)	**23** (A) (B) (C) (D)
4 (A) (B) (C) (D)	**14** (A) (B) (C) (D)	**24** (A) (B) (C) (D)
5 (A) (B) (C) (D)	**15** (A) (B) (C) (D)	**25** (A) (B) (C) (D)
6 (A) (B) (C) (D)	**16** (A) (B) (C) (D)	**26** (A) (B) (C) (D)
7 (A) (B) (C) (D)	**17** (A) (B) (C) (D)	**27** (A) (B) (C) (D)
8 (A) (B) (C) (D)	**18** (A) (B) (C) (D)	**28** (A) (B) (C) (D)
9 (A) (B) (C) (D)	**19** (A) (B) (C) (D)	**29** (A) (B) (C) (D)
10 (A) (B) (C) (D)	**20** (A) (B) (C) (D)	**30** (A) (B) (C) (D)

Student Name: _____ Grade Applying For: _____

Write in blue or black pen for this essay

Write your essay topic below

_____

_____

_____

Write your essay below and on the next page

_____

_____

_____

_____

_____

_____

_____

_____

_____

_____

_____

_____

_____

_____

_____

_____

_____

_____

_____

_____

_____

Practice Test 2

Section 1: Verbal Reasoning

1 (A) (B) (C) (D)	13 (A) (B) (C) (D)	24 (A) (B) (C) (D)
2 (A) (B) (C) (D)	14 (A) (B) (C) (D)	25 (A) (B) (C) (D)
3 (A) (B) (C) (D)	15 (A) (B) (C) (D)	26 (A) (B) (C) (D)
4 (A) (B) (C) (D)	16 (A) (B) (C) (D)	27 (A) (B) (C) (D)
5 (A) (B) (C) (D)	17 (A) (B) (C) (D)	28 (A) (B) (C) (D)
6 (A) (B) (C) (D)	18 (A) (B) (C) (D)	29 (A) (B) (C) (D)
7 (A) (B) (C) (D)	19 (A) (B) (C) (D)	30 (A) (B) (C) (D)
8 (A) (B) (C) (D)	20 (A) (B) (C) (D)	31 (A) (B) (C) (D)
9 (A) (B) (C) (D)	21 (A) (B) (C) (D)	32 (A) (B) (C) (D)
10 (A) (B) (C) (D)	22 (A) (B) (C) (D)	33 (A) (B) (C) (D)
11 (A) (B) (C) (D)	23 (A) (B) (C) (D)	34 (A) (B) (C) (D)
12 (A) (B) (C) (D)		

Section 2: Quantitative Reasoning

1 (A) (B) (C) (D)	14 (A) (B) (C) (D)	27 (A) (B) (C) (D)
2 (A) (B) (C) (D)	15 (A) (B) (C) (D)	28 (A) (B) (C) (D)
3 (A) (B) (C) (D)	16 (A) (B) (C) (D)	29 (A) (B) (C) (D)
4 (A) (B) (C) (D)	17 (A) (B) (C) (D)	30 (A) (B) (C) (D)
5 (A) (B) (C) (D)	18 (A) (B) (C) (D)	31 (A) (B) (C) (D)
6 (A) (B) (C) (D)	19 (A) (B) (C) (D)	32 (A) (B) (C) (D)
7 (A) (B) (C) (D)	20 (A) (B) (C) (D)	33 (A) (B) (C) (D)
8 (A) (B) (C) (D)	21 (A) (B) (C) (D)	34 (A) (B) (C) (D)
9 (A) (B) (C) (D)	22 (A) (B) (C) (D)	35 (A) (B) (C) (D)
10 (A) (B) (C) (D)	23 (A) (B) (C) (D)	36 (A) (B) (C) (D)
11 (A) (B) (C) (D)	24 (A) (B) (C) (D)	37 (A) (B) (C) (D)
12 (A) (B) (C) (D)	25 (A) (B) (C) (D)	38 (A) (B) (C) (D)
13 (A) (B) (C) (D)	26 (A) (B) (C) (D)	

Section 3: Reading Comprehension

1 (A) (B) (C) (D)	**10** (A) (B) (C) (D)	**18** (A) (B) (C) (D)
2 (A) (B) (C) (D)	**11** (A) (B) (C) (D)	**19** (A) (B) (C) (D)
3 (A) (B) (C) (D)	**12** (A) (B) (C) (D)	**20** (A) (B) (C) (D)
4 (A) (B) (C) (D)	**13** (A) (B) (C) (D)	**21** (A) (B) (C) (D)
5 (A) (B) (C) (D)	**14** (A) (B) (C) (D)	**22** (A) (B) (C) (D)
6 (A) (B) (C) (D)	**15** (A) (B) (C) (D)	**23** (A) (B) (C) (D)
7 (A) (B) (C) (D)	**16** (A) (B) (C) (D)	**24** (A) (B) (C) (D)
8 (A) (B) (C) (D)	**17** (A) (B) (C) (D)	**25** (A) (B) (C) (D)
9 (A) (B) (C) (D)		

Section 4: Mathematics Achievement

1 (A) (B) (C) (D)	**11** (A) (B) (C) (D)	**21** (A) (B) (C) (D)
2 (A) (B) (C) (D)	**12** (A) (B) (C) (D)	**22** (A) (B) (C) (D)
3 (A) (B) (C) (D)	**13** (A) (B) (C) (D)	**23** (A) (B) (C) (D)
4 (A) (B) (C) (D)	**14** (A) (B) (C) (D)	**24** (A) (B) (C) (D)
5 (A) (B) (C) (D)	**15** (A) (B) (C) (D)	**25** (A) (B) (C) (D)
6 (A) (B) (C) (D)	**16** (A) (B) (C) (D)	**26** (A) (B) (C) (D)
7 (A) (B) (C) (D)	**17** (A) (B) (C) (D)	**27** (A) (B) (C) (D)
8 (A) (B) (C) (D)	**18** (A) (B) (C) (D)	**28** (A) (B) (C) (D)
9 (A) (B) (C) (D)	**19** (A) (B) (C) (D)	**29** (A) (B) (C) (D)
10 (A) (B) (C) (D)	**20** (A) (B) (C) (D)	**30** (A) (B) (C) (D)

Student Name: _____ Grade Applying For: _____

Write in blue or black pen for this essay

Write your essay topic below

_____

_____

_____

Write your essay below and on the next page

_____

_____

_____

_____

_____

_____

_____

_____

_____

_____

_____

_____

_____

_____

_____

_____

_____

_____

_____

_____

_____

Practice Test 1

Verbal Reasoning

34 questions
20 minutes

Part One — Synonyms

Directions: For each question, a word is given in capital letters. Select the answer choice that has the word that is closest in meaning to the word given in capital letters.

1. MODEST:

   (A) humble
   (B) natural
   (C) poisonous
   (D) slippery

2. HUSTLE:

   (A) embarrass
   (B) flutter
   (C) mention
   (D) rush

3. TRICKLE:

   (A) accept
   (B) dribble
   (C) pity
   (D) shriek

4. MIMIC:

   (A) copy
   (B) lead
   (C) poke
   (D) spread

CONTINUE TO THE NEXT PAGE

5. COMPACT:

   (A) busy
   (B) honest
   (C) small
   (D) vacant

6. SINCERE:

   (A) definite
   (B) earnest
   (C) obedient
   (D) severe

7. BIZARRE:

   (A) dingy
   (B) innocent
   (C) occasional
   (D) strange

8. SCHEME:

   (A) ditch
   (B) interview
   (C) plan
   (D) tradition

9. DILUTE:

   (A) agree
   (B) exchange
   (C) thrill
   (D) weaken

10. CHERISH:

   (A) fade
   (B) juggle
   (C) treasure
   (D) wrench

CONTINUE TO THE NEXT PAGE

11. ENLIGHTEN:

   (A) educate
   (B) gossip
   (C) label
   (D) shrug

12. IMMENSE:

   (A) huge
   (B) jealous
   (C) moody
   (D) sheltered

13. EXHAUSTED:

   (A) prompt
   (B) tired
   (C) wistful
   (D) wretched

14. SPARSE:

   (A) alienated
   (B) discontent
   (C) sour
   (D) thin

15. CREVICE:

   (A) balm
   (B) hint
   (C) opening
   (D) surplus

16. TEMPERATE:

   (A) fractured
   (B) mild
   (C) sacred
   (D) sympathetic

CONTINUE TO THE NEXT PAGE

17. CHRONIC:

(A) lingering
(B) monotone
(C) quaint
(D) stale

Part Two- Sentence Completions

Directions: Choose the answer that best completes the meaning of the sentence.

18. Looking at the ------- landscape of the Sahara desert it is easy to see why it is so hard for life to exist there.

(A) active
(B) desolate
(C) precious
(D) thriving

19. Frank Lloyd Wright was an architect well-known for his use of ------- materials such as stone, wood, and running water.

(A) gathered
(B) helpful
(C) natural
(D) shallow

20. A significant risk for marine life is the floating ------ in our oceans such as old plastic bottles, bags, and other packaging.

(A) debris
(B) interior
(C) remedies
(D) science

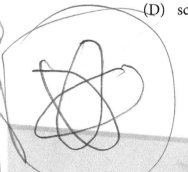

CONTINUE TO THE NEXT PAGE

21. Even if the ground around a house seems to be perfectly flat, it often has a subtle --------- away from the house so that water will not be directed toward the house.

   (A) basement
   (B) explanation
   (C) review
   (D) slant

22. In a remarkable display of --------, Abraham Lincoln continued to run for office despite losing several elections and eventually became the 16th president of the United States.

   (A) determination
   (B) fury
   (C) popularity
   (D) respect

23. Before getting a driver's license a person must ------- that they have good vision, knowledge of the laws of the road, and the ability to drive safely.

   (A) experience
   (B) demonstrate
   (C) disprove
   (D) retreat

24. When the students were -------, the teacher had to cancel the fieldtrip and tell the bus driver to return them to school.

   (A) darling
   (B) fortunate
   (C) unruly
   (D) warm

CONTINUE TO THE NEXT PAGE

25. Although Claire was known for being rude to strangers, she was actually quite -------- when she met the new instructor.

(A) abrupt
(B) cordial
(C) rebellious
(D) vivid

26. A common ------- for new business owners is that they underestimate how much time and money a project will take to complete.

(A) advantage
(B) division
(C) interest
(D) pitfall

27. Benjamin Franklin was known for his -------- ways, refusing to spend any more money than absolutely necessary.

(A) frugal
(B) graceful
(C) reasonable
(D) suspicious

28. Although many politicians often promise ------ when they are campaigning, when those same people take office they find that change is slow and hard to accomplish as an elected official.

(A) citizenship
(B) inaction
(C) reform
(D) tolerance

29. Most swimmers retire in their twenties, but Dara Torres --------.

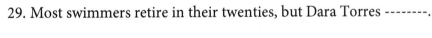

(A) set many records as a teenager
(B) was selected for the U.S. Olympic swim team at age 41
(C) overcame many injuries
(D) missed important tryouts

CONTINUE TO THE NEXT PAGE

30. Since many students missed the announcement about afterschool activities being cancelled, they were -------.

(A) surprised when there was no band practice after school
(B) able to go directly home
(C) encouraged to sign up for a sport
(D) absent during the school day

31. Unlike Nellie, who struggled with completing her work without help, Tomas --------.

(A) frequently had to be assisted
(B) had always liked school
(C) was a poor student
(D) excelled at working independently

32. Even though Mark Twain earned a lot of money from his books and lectures, at one point in his life --------.

(A) he was considered a great author
(B) he was wealthy
(C) he could not repay the people that he owed money to
(D) he was not yet a published writer

33. While Davy Crockett was known for being an outdoorsmen while he was alive, after his death -------.

(A) his wilderness skills became legendary
(B) he was a congressman
(C) he was buried
(D) there was much controversy

34. Because of a drought in the American West in the 1930's, many farmers -------.

(A) grew wheat and corn
(B) had to move away from their farms
(C) were related to one another
(D) donated to charities

STOP

IF YOU HAVE TIME LEFT YOU MAY CHECK YOUR ANSWERS IN THIS SECTION ONLY

Quantitative Reasoning

38 questions

35 minutes

Directions: Each of the following math questions has four possible answers after it. Choose the correct answer for the question.

1. Harriet has a bouquet of 36 flowers. If 9 of them are carnations, what fraction of the flowers are carnations?

   (A) $\frac{1}{4}$

   (B) $\frac{1}{3}$

   (C) $\frac{1}{2}$

   (D) $\frac{2}{3}$

2. Marsha has to buy candy bars for a campfire. She needs a total of 48 candy bars and there are 6 candy bars in a package. Which calculation would help her figure out how packages she needs to buy?

   (A) $48 + 6$
   (B) $48 - 6$
   (C) 48×6
   (D) $48 \div 6$

3. Manny is thinking of a whole number that is greater than 6 but less than 13. It is also greater than 2 but less than 8. What is the number that Manny is thinking of?

   (A) 5
   (B) 6
   (C) 7
   (D) 8

CONTINUE TO THE NEXT PAGE

4. Which equation represents the commutative property?

(A) $3(2 + 5) = (3 \times 2) + (3 \times 5)$
(B) $3 + 2 = 2 + 3$
(C) $(3 + 2) + 5 = 3 + (2 + 5)$
(D) $3(2 + 5) = (3 \times 2) \times (3 \times 5)$

5. A rectangle has an area of 36 cm^2. Which of the following could be its dimensions?

(A) $2 \text{ cm} \times 16 \text{ cm}$
(B) $4 \text{ cm} \times 9 \text{ cm}$
(C) $5 \text{ cm} \times 6 \text{ cm}$
(D) $6 \text{ cm} \times 8 \text{ cm}$

6. All of the following are true EXCEPT

(A) $\dfrac{1}{3} = \dfrac{12}{27}$

(B) $\dfrac{1}{2} = \dfrac{6}{12}$

(C) $\dfrac{2}{5} = \dfrac{10}{25}$

(D) $\dfrac{3}{4} = \dfrac{12}{16}$

7. Use the equations below.

$$4 + m = 8$$
$$3 + n = 8$$

What is the value of $m + n$?

(A) 3
(B) 4
(C) 5
(D) 9

CONTINUE TO THE NEXT PAGE

8. Use the figure below to answer the question.

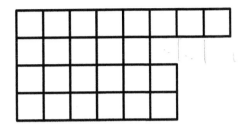

Which piece would complete the figure to make a rectangle?

(A)

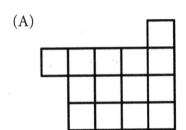

(B)

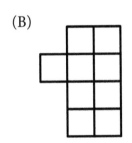

(C)

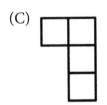

(D)

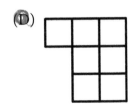

CONTINUE TO THE NEXT PAGE

9. Use the figure below to answer the question.

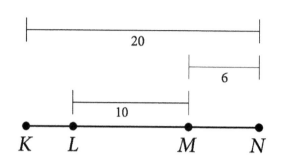

Based on the figure above, what is the length of segment *KL*?

(A) 2
(B) 4
(C) 6
(D) 8

10. Which fraction has the least value?

(A) $\dfrac{6}{11}$

(B) $\dfrac{7}{13}$

(C) $\dfrac{8}{16}$

(D) $\dfrac{9}{17}$

11. Jakob and Clancy are running at the same speed. If it takes Jakob 24 minutes to run 3 miles, then how many minutes will it take Clancy to run 4 miles?

(A) 32
(B) 36
(C) 42
(D) 48

CONTINUE TO THE NEXT PAGE

12. If a number can be divided by both 2 and 5 without a remainder, then what other number can it also be divided by without a remainder?

   (A) 3
   (B) 10
   (C) 15
   (D) 18

13. Refer to the Venn Diagram to answer the question.

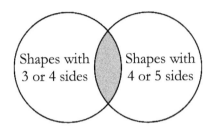

   Which of the following could be found in the shaded region?

   (A) blue triangles
   (B) green octagons
   (C) red pentagons
   (D) yellow rectangles

14. Which number represents four thousand thirty-two?

   (A) 4,023
   (B) 4,032
   (C) 4,230
   (D) 4,302

15. What is the best way to estimate the answer to 3.89×5.14 ?

   (A) 3×5
   (B) 3×6
   (C) 4×5
   (D) 4×6

CONTINUE TO THE NEXT PAGE

16. Nora went back-to-school shopping for supplies. The table below shows the items that she bought.

Supplies	Price for 1 item	Total spent on that item
Pencils	$0.05	$1.00
Pack of paper	$1.25	$2.50
Binder	$2.50	$7.50
Erasers	$0.10	?

If Nora spent a total of $11.50 on school supplies, how many erasers did she buy?

(A) 2
(B) 3
(C) 4
(D) 5

17. If the perimeter of an equilateral triangle is $6w$, then what is the length of one side?

(A) 2
(B) 3
(C) $2w$
(D) $3w$

18. If $12 = 2x + 2$, then what is the value of x?

(A) 5
(B) 6
(C) 10
(D) 12

CONTINUE TO THE NEXT PAGE

19. Use the input/output table below to answer the question.

Input x	Output y
3	6
8	11
9	12
12	15

What is the rule for this function?

(A) $x \times 2 = y$
(B) $x + 3 = y$
(C) $(3 \times x) - 3 = y$
(D) $4 \times x = y$

20. Elisa has a bag with 30 marbles in it. There are 4 red marbles, 12 green marbles, 6 yellow marbles, and the rest are blue. If Elisa were to randomly pick a marble from her bag, which color has a 4 in 15 chance of being chosen?

(A) red
(B) green
(C) yellow
(D) blue

21. Refer to the figure below to answer the question.

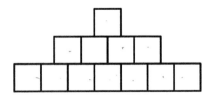

If one more row of squares is added to the figure following the same pattern, how many squares would be in the fourth row?

(A) 7
(B) 8
(C) 9
(D) 10

CONTINUE TO THE NEXT PAGE

22. Use the pattern below.

$$2 + 4 = 2 \times 3$$
$$2 + 4 + 6 = 3 \times 4$$
$$2 + 4 + 6 + 8 = 4 \times 5$$

What is $2 + 4 + 6 + 8 + 10 + 12 + 14 + 16$?

(A) 8×9
(B) 8×16
(C) 2×16
(D) 5×6

23. Use the graph below to answer the question.

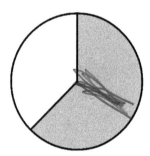

If the shaded portion of the graph above represents 30 students, then how many students are represented by the unshaded portion?

(A) 18
(B) 30
(C) 50
(D) 80

24. A class was recording the rainfall for each month in their town. They recorded 2.0 inches, 4.0 inches, 3.0 inches, 3.5 inches, and 4.0 inches for five different months. What is the median of this data?

(A) 2.0 inches
(B) 3.3 inches
(C) 3.5 inches
(D) 4.0 inches

CONTINUE TO THE NEXT PAGE

25. Use the number line below to answer the question.

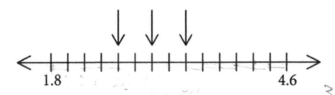

1.8   4.6

Which three numbers are the arrows pointing to?

(A) 2.0, 3.0, 4.0
(B) 2.2, 2.4, 2.6
(C) 2.6, 3.0, 3.4
(D) 2.8, 3.4, 4.0

26. Rodney bought two pairs of pants that cost $10 each and a shirt. He spent a total of $35. Which equation would allow Rodney to figure out the cost of the shirt (s)?

(A) $10 + s = 35$
(B) $10 + 2s = 35$
(C) $20 + s = 35$
(D) $20 + 2s = 35$

27. Use the figure below to answer the question.

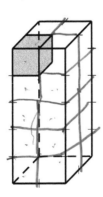

The volume of the shaded cube is 1 cm^3. What is the volume of the rectangular prism?

(A) 10 cm^3
(B) 20 cm^3
(C) 40 cm^3
(D) 125 cm^3

CONTINUE TO THE NEXT PAGE

28. Bob has red, blue, and green candies. He has twice as many red candies as blue candies. He has three times as many green candies as red candies. If he has a total of 9 candies, how many red candies does he have?

(A) 1
(B) 2
(C) 3
(D) 6

29. Refer to the figure below to answer the question.

A B C

If the length of AC is p and the length of BC is q, then what is the length of AB?

(A) $2p$
(B) $2q$
(C) $p + q$
(D) $p - q$

30. Domingo was making fruit punch for his friends. He combined the following ingredients and then equally divided the punch among 6 glasses.

INGREDIENTS
4 cups apple juice
3 cups orange juice
4 cups cranberry juice
3 cups pineapple juice

How many cups of juice were poured into each of the glasses?

(A) $2\frac{1}{3}$

(B) $2\frac{1}{2}$

(C) 3

(D) $3\frac{1}{3}$

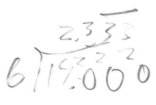

CONTINUE TO THE NEXT PAGE

31. Use the figure below.

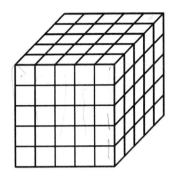

How many small cubes are needed to make the large cube?

(A) 5
(B) 25
(C) 125
(D) 500

32. Mr. Wilkins has black and white plastic chips in a bag. If he randomly picks a chip out of the bag, the probability that he would choose a white chip is 4 out of 7. There are 12 black chips in the bag. How many white chips are there in the bag?

(A) 12
(B) 13
(C) 14
(D) 16

CONTINUE TO THE NEXT PAGE

33. Use the graph below to answer the question.

Boxes of cookies sold

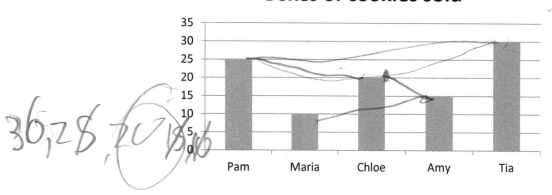

Based on the graph above, which of the following statements is true?

(A) The mean is 15.
(B) The median is 20.
(C) The range is 25.
(D) Tia sold twice as many cookies as Chloe.

34. Use the figures below to answer the question.

Figure 1

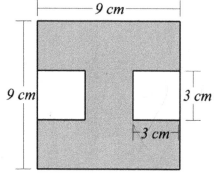

Figure 2

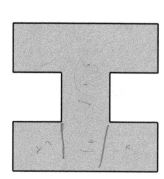

Figure 1 shows a 9-cm square. Two 3-cm squares are removed to leave the shape shown in Figure 2. What is the area of the shape shown in Figure 2?

(A) 12 cm²
(B) 36 cm²
(C) 63 cm²
(D) 99 cm²

CONTINUE TO THE NEXT PAGE

35. The coordinate points $(-3, 2)$, $(-3, 4)$, $(1, 4)$ and $(1, 2)$ are connected to form a quadrilateral. Which term is the best description of this quadrilateral?

(A) rectangle
(B) rhombus
(C) square
(D) trapezoid

36. If Y is divided by 4, the remainder is 2. What would the remainder be when $3Y$ is divided by 4?

(A) 1
(B) 2
(C) 3
(D) 4

37. Which of the following is a pair of letters with an equal number of lines of symmetry?

(A)

(B)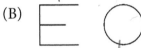

(C)

(D)

38. A scale on a map says that 1.4 inches represents 20 miles. How many inches would be used to represent 50 miles?

(A) 1.8
(B) 2.8
(C) 3.5
(D) 4.8

STOP

IF YOU HAVE TIME LEFT YOU MAY CHECK YOUR ANSWERS IN THIS SECTION ONLY

Reading Comprehension

25 questions

25 minutes

Directions: The reading comprehension section has five passages. Each passage has five questions after it. For each question, choose the answer that best reflects what is either implied or stated in the passage.

Questions #1-5

1   In most other countries around the world soccer is called fútbol. Soccer, or fútbol,
2 is the most popular sport in the world. Every four years, fútbol teams from around the
3 world represent their countries and compete in the World Cup. This is considered the
4 world championship of soccer. More than nine hundred million people watched the
5 World Cup final in 2010, making it one of the most popular sporting events in the world.
6   The first World Cup was in 1930. Thirteen teams participated. A man from
7 France, named Jules Rimet, was very important to organizing the first tournament. In
8 his honor, the World Cup Trophy is named after him.
9   For a long time when a country won the World Cup, they got to keep the trophy
10 forever. The original versions of the trophy were made of solid gold. Because solid gold
11 is very valuable, the cup was stolen two times. The last time a World Cup was stolen
12 was in Brazil in 1983. The thieves melted the trophy so that they could make more
13 money when they sold the gold. Now, the trophy no longer stays with the winning team
14 forever. It travels to the winning country of the next World Cup. Teams get to keep a
15 version of the trophy that it is not made of solid gold.
16   The World Cup only happens once every four years. Therefore, the players play
17 on professional soccer teams around the world when they are not playing in the World
18 Cup. Then, when it is time for the World Cup, they join the teams of their home
19 countries and compete, much like what happens during the Olympic games.
20   Women's soccer teams had their first World Cup in 1991, over sixty years after the
21 first men's World Cup. The women's World Cup happens two years after the men's
22 World Cup. This way soccer and fútbol fans around the world have an exciting event
23 to look forward to every two years.

CONTINUE TO THE NEXT PAGE

1. The main purpose of this passage is to

   (A) explain why soccer is called fútbol in many countries.
   (B) detail why winning teams don't get to keep the trophy forever.
   (C) share interesting facts about the World Cup.
   (D) discuss the rules of soccer.

2. The passage states which of the following about the World Cup?

   (A) The trophy is named after Jules Rimet.
   (B) The first women's competition was in 1983.
   (C) Countries currently get to keep the trophy forever.
   (D) It happens every year.

3. According to the passage, how often can fans watch either a men's or women's World Cup tournament?

   (A) every year
   (B) every two years
   (C) every four years
   (D) every six years

4. Which question could be answered by information in the passage?

   (A) Where was the first World Cup held?
   (B) What is the second most popular sport?
   (C) Who won the first women's World Cup?
   (D) Is gold valuable?

5. The passage implies that teams no longer get to keep the World Cup trophy forever because

   (A) countries prefer to keep a copy.
   (B) the material used to make the real trophy is too valuable.
   (C) the World Cup is played every four years.
   (D) soccer is called fútbol in some countries.

CONTINUE TO THE NEXT PAGE

1   Do you ever wonder where the food on your plate comes from? Many important
2 processes take place before your food is shipped to the grocery store. The growing
3 process is called the crop cycle. Three of the most important steps of the crop cycle are
4 planting the seeds, allowing the crops to grow, and then harvesting the crops.

5   Before farmers plant any seeds, they must first make sure the land is ready. The
6 land has to be well-watered and tilled so that plants can grow roots into the soil. It is
7 also important that farmers pick the right time of year to plant their seeds and pay close
8 attention to the weather. For example, it is best to plant corn between February and
9 April. Different seeds are planted at different times of year, though.

10   Once the seeds are planted, the crops will begin to grow. Crop growth is the longest
11 part of the farming process. During crop growth, farmers must take care of their fields
12 and watch out for anything that might harm the crops. Farmers must keep an eye out
13 for things like weeds, bugs, or animals that are eating the crops, and weather conditions
14 that could kill or harm the crops. The length of the crop growth part of the cycle varies
15 tremendously. A crop of corn takes between two or three months to fully grow.

16   The harvest is the last step for farmers. After crops are fully grown, farmers harvest
17 the crops to pick the food from the crop and sell it. Sometimes this is just like you going
18 out to pick an apple from a tree, but for most farmers it involves using big machines and
19 many weeks of work. Farmers must harvest crops at the right time in order to maximize
20 the yield. It is also important for farmers to properly store and transport the crop once
21 it is harvested.

22   After the harvest is finished, farmers look to start the crop cycle again. The work
23 farmers do is very important because it helps get food from the ground to your dinner
24 table.

CONTINUE TO THE NEXT PAGE

6. Which title would best express the main idea of this passage?

   (A) Keeping Crops Safe from Insects and Weeds
   (B) The Right Time of Year to Plant Corn
   (C) Crop Cycle: How Our Food is Grown
   (D) The Importance of Family Farms

7. The primary purpose of the first paragraph (lines 1-4) is to

   (A) explain to the reader why the crop cycle is important.
   (B) create a sense of suspense for the reader.
   (C) provide details about the first step in the crop cycle.
   (D) introduce the author's background.

8. In line 20 the word "yield" refers to

   (A) seeds.
   (B) the crop cycle.
   (C) the time it takes to harvest the crop.
   (D) the amount of food gathered from the harvest.

9. In the third paragraph (lines 10-15), the passages implies that weeds

   (A) are always deadly to crops.
   (B) need to be managed during crop growth.
   (C) make harvesting difficult.
   (D) affect the length of the crop growth stage.

10. The passage implies that farmers

   (A) are generally engaged in some stage of the crop cycle most of the time.
   (B) are not concerned with seed selection.
   (C) usually pick the crops by hand.
   (D) don't have to plan around the weather for planting.

CONTINUE TO THE NEXT PAGE

1   For all of us who care about the safety, beauty, and convenience of living in a small
2 town, it is imperative that we vote against the proposed widening of Main Street. The
3 village council has already agreed to look at plans for turning our two-lane road into
4 four lanes. Now is the time for concerned citizens to fight this decision before it's too
5 late. Before you head to the polls next Thursday, consider the impact this change would
6 have on our town.

7   Main Street is not only used by cars, but also by cyclists. Widening the road to four
8 lanes would make biking on Main Street difficult and possibly even deadly for cyclists.
9 In order to widen the road, city planners intend to eliminate the existing bike lane. This
10 would leave no room for cyclists to safely share the road. Even if they switched to using
11 the sidewalk, which presents its own problems, the increased traffic would make it more
12 difficult and dangerous to cross intersections.

13   Another problem with the proposed widening of Main Street is the negative effect
14 it will have on our picturesque village. Increasing the number of lanes will mean adding
15 more traffic signals and signs. We already have strict limits on businesses putting up
16 signs in our town center and these restrictions should apply to traffic signs as well. No
17 one wants our historic, welcoming town center marred by flashing lights, large signs,
18 and a tangle of cables.

19   Finally, the lane increase will turn our calm, convenient Main Street into a traffic
20 nightmare. The city planners are claiming that the construction will improve the flow
21 of traffic. Creating four lanes is an invitation for commuters to flock to this route when
22 traveling between Johnsonville and West Concord, however. The speed limit will be
23 increased as well, so we will have a larger volume of high-speed traffic moving right
24 through the middle of our town. Keeping Main Street two lanes wide allows us to
25 maintain a lower speed limit and accommodate just the local traffic. The residents who
26 live here in town want to be able to drive or bike to the Main Street shops without facing
27 rush hour traffic jams.

28   Please consider the negative effects of the Main Street plan when you go to vote
29 next Thursday. Think of the children riding their bikes to Ganci's Sweet Shop or the
30 elderly drivers headed to the senior center. Consider your own enjoyment of our
31 beautiful and safe town center. Then, please join me in voting NO to the expansion of
32 Main Street.

CONTINUE TO THE NEXT PAGE

11. The author of this passage objects to widening Main Street for all of the following reasons EXCEPT

   (A) the safety of cyclists.
   (B) the volume of traffic through the center of town.
   (C) elderly drivers going to Ganci's Sweet Shop.
   (D) the speed of drivers travelling through the town center.

12. In line 25 the word "accommodate" most nearly means

   (A) limit
   (B) allow for
   (C) invite
   (D) dismiss

13. It can be inferred from the passage that Main Street

   (A) exists in a large city.
   (B) is currently four lanes wide.
   (C) has a high speed limit.
   (D) runs between Johnsonville and West Concord.

14. The primary purpose of this passage is to

   (A) explain a recent change.
   (B) convince the readers to take a certain action.
   (C) list the advantages and disadvantages of a suggested change.
   (D) describe one person's experiences.

15. The final paragraph (lines 28-32) can best be described as

   (A) an emotional appeal.
   (B) a summary of the passage.
   (C) a contradiction of earlier points.
   (D) an exciting finish.

CONTINUE TO THE NEXT PAGE

1   My mysterious encounter with the disappearing crab began like most other days. I
2 had gotten to the building while it was still dark out. Only one other car sat in the parking
3 lot – most likely belonging to the reclusive librarian, who usually needed at least one cup
4 of coffee before socializing with colleagues. I unlocked the classroom door and turned on
5 just the first row of lights. Little did I know the excitement that was to come.

6   As I set my briefcase down next to my chair, I eyed the stack of papers that needed
7 grading. I had every intention of doing just that, but, as I hung up my coat, a strange
8 sensation caused me to change my mind. I'm not sure if I had somehow sensed something
9 wrong, but a feeling inside urged me to check on the class pet.

10   I strode across the room to the back counter where Kermit's tank resided. At first
11 glance, there was no hermit crab to be seen. This was not yet surprising, as Kermit is a
12 master of illusion. I walked away to turn on the rest of the lights and came back to take a
13 better look. Still, no Kermit. I turned over the piece of dead branch and raked my fingers
14 through the wood chips. No luck. This was becoming mysterious, indeed.

15   I scanned the glass tank and the surrounding area. Could he have gotten out? How?
16 The branch was not high enough to reach the top of the tank and nothing else showed any
17 sign of disturbance. Can hermit crabs jump? I didn't think so. The classroom sink was
18 next to Kermit's tank. Could he have gotten down the drain? That would certainly be a
19 problem. The radiator vents opened through the back of the counter. What if he had
20 somehow gotten into there? I didn't like to consider his chances of survival once the heat
21 kicked on, if that was the case.

22   Just then, as I was picturing various worst-case scenarios, I heard the sounds of my
23 first students arriving. I would have to think quickly. There would be questions. They
24 would demand answers! My eyes darted to the job chart on the bulletin board. Whose
25 turn was it to feed Kermit this week? Aha! It was Salim and he had been absent for three
26 days. Maybe he wouldn't show up today looking to feed the hermit crab that wasn't there.

27   As my heart raced and palms sweated, the students filed in like any other morning.
28 There were no questions. There were no curious faces peering in to the empty tank. The
29 announcements came on and we eased into our day. I had actually forgotten all about
30 our disappearing hermit crab as I began writing multiplication problems on the
31 chalkboard. Lost in mathematical thoughts, my concentration was suddenly broken by a
32 piercing scream.

33   I spun around to see Olivia reeling back from the counter and a tissue box falling to
34 the floor. To everyone else in the room, this was a startling and incomprehensible chain
35 of events. But as for me, I knew exactly what must have happened. I just couldn't seem
36 to figure out how it had happened.

CONTINUE TO THE NEXT PAGE

16. The main purpose of this passage is to

(A) inform readers about the characteristics of hermit crabs.
(B) explain how to care for hermit crabs.
(C) describe what happened on one school day.
(D) criticize one student.

17. It can be inferred from the passage that Olivia screamed because

(A) a tissue box fell.
(B) Salim scared her.
(C) the heat came on.
(D) she found Kermit.

18. The author implies that Kermit

(A) often hides.
(B) is good at jumping.
(C) belongs in another classroom.
(D) doesn't like hot places.

19. The author's attitude toward Kermit's escape can best be described as

(A) anger.
(B) puzzlement.
(C) sorrow.
(D) triumphant.

20. It can be inferred from the passage that the author is most likely

(A) a student.
(B) a principal.
(C) a teacher.
(D) a parent.

CONTINUE TO THE NEXT PAGE

1   In the United States, we celebrate the birthday of Martin Luther King, Jr. He
2 fought for equal rights for all Americans during the 1950s and 1960s. Many people do
3 not know that Dr. King was greatly influenced by a man who lived halfway around the
4 world. Mohandas K. Ghandi lived in India and spoke about peaceful conflict resolution.
5 Peaceful conflict resolution became a guiding principle for Dr. King.

6   Ghandi was also known as "Mahatma", a title that means "venerable". He fought
7 against the British occupation of India in the first half of the 20th century. He taught the
8 spirit of noncooperation and peaceful resistance and opposed violent rebellion.

9   The goal of the Noncooperation Movement in India was to establish an
10 independent government, or *swaraj*. Ghandi was also in favor of freedom for all people.
11 He fought for greater rights for women and the elimination of the caste system. In India,
12 the caste system separated citizens into strict groups. One group was considered
13 untouchable and had no civil rights.

14   Just as Ghandi fought for the rights of the untouchables, Dr. King fought for equal
15 rights for African-American citizens. Dr. King also did not advocate violence. He
16 encouraged protesters to remain peaceful but to resist being removed. Ghandi's
17 Noncooperation Movement had helped India win independence from Britain. Dr. King
18 hoped to gain civil rights for African-Americans using the same methods.

19   Tragically, both Dr. King and Mahatma Gandhi were assassinated. We honor both
20 Dr. King and Mahatma Gandhi whenever we choose to end disagreements with a
21 peaceful resolution.

CONTINUE TO THE NEXT PAGE

21. The main idea of this passage is

    (A) that both Dr. King and Mahatma Ghandi taught nonviolent protest.
    (B) the importance of celebrating Dr. King's birthday.
    (C) Ghandi's contribution to women's rights.
    (D) the history of nonviolence.

22. The passage states that untouchables were

    (A) against *swaraj*.
    (B) a group in America.
    (C) in favor of nonviolence.
    (D) a group of people without civil rights.

23. In line 12 the word "strict" is closest in meaning to

    (A) loyal.
    (B) messy.
    (C) unbendable.
    (D) violent.

24. According to the passage, how can we honor both Dr. King and Ghandi?

    (A) Celebrate their birthdays every year.
    (B) Solve disputes without violence.
    (C) Practice different religions.
    (D) Fight against civil rights.

25. Which question could be answered with information from the passage?

    (A) What was the caste system?
    (B) How long did Ghandi live?
    (C) Was Dr. King successful?
    (D) When was Dr. King born?

STOP

IF YOU HAVE TIME LEFT YOU MAY CHECK YOUR ANSWERS IN THIS SECTION ONLY

Mathematics Achievement

30 minutes

30 questions

Directions: Each of the following math questions has four possible answers after it. Choose the correct answer for the question.

1. Which number can be divided by 4 without leaving a remainder?

   (A) 14
   (B) 20
   (C) 30
   (D) 34

2. Use the figure below.

   Ms. Swanson's classroom

   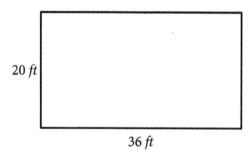

   20 ft

   36 ft

   Based on the figure above, what is the perimeter of Ms. Swanson's classroom?

   (A) 56 ft
   (B) 76 ft
   (C) 112 ft
   (D) 720 ft

CONTINUE TO THE NEXT PAGE

3. Marley had 32 candies in a bag. She gave 7 candies to Tim and 8 candies to Sarah. How many candies did Marley have left in her bag?

(A) 17
(B) 20
(C) 24
(D) 25

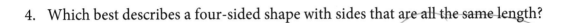

4. Which best describes a four-sided shape with sides that are all the same length?

(A) triangle
(B) hexagon
(C) pentagon
(D) rhombus

5. Which statement correctly represents 304,052?

(A) three hundred forty thousand fifty-two
(B) three hundred four thousand five hundred two
(C) three hundred four thousand fifty-two
(D) three hundred four thousand five hundred twenty

6. Which is equal to $2 \times (6 - 3 + 5)$?

(A) 14
(B) 16
(C) 20
(D) 24

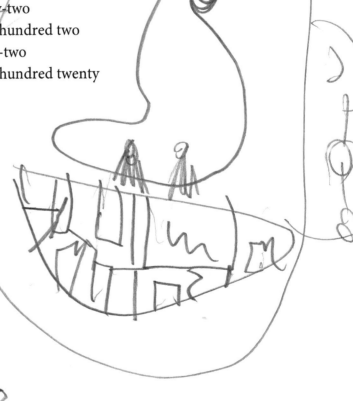

7. What is the result of $409 - 51$?

(A) 358
(B) 363
(C) 368
(D) 373

CONTINUE TO THE NEXT PAGE

8. Use the number line below to answer the question.

A

23   41

What number is represented by point *A*?

(A) 23.5
(B) 24
(C) 24.5
(D) 25

9. For a period of 5 days, an elementary school kept track of how many students got to school each day by walking, being driven in a car, and riding the bus. The chart below shows the data.

	# of students walking	# of students driven in a car	# of students riding the bus
Day #1	50	60	100
Day #2	55	62	93
Day #3	61	59	90
Day #4	68	63	79
Day #5	76	58	76

On Day #4, how many more students rode the bus than were driven in a car?

(A) 11
(B) 16
(C) 18
(D) 79

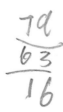

10. Which decimal is equal to $\frac{2}{100}$?

(A) 0.0002
(B) 0.002
(C) 0.02
(D) 0.2

CONTINUE TO THE NEXT PAGE

11. For what value of M will the equation $M + M + M + M = M \times M$ be true?

    (A) 1
    (B) 2
    (C) 3
    (D) 4

12. What does $3 \times (\boxdot + 4)$ equal if $\boxdot$ is equal to 5?

$3 \times (5 + 4)$

    (A) 19
    (B) 27
    (C) 36
    (D) 40

13. A wheelbarrow can hold up to 100 pounds. If Bob wants to move stones that weigh 8 pounds each, what is the largest number of stones that he can put in the wheelbarrow?

    (A) 12
    (B) 13
    (C) 14
    (D) 15

14. If $\dfrac{5}{8} = \dfrac{\boxdot}{32}$, then what does $\boxdot$ equal?

    (A) 20
    (B) 24
    (C) 28
    (D) 30

CONTINUE TO THE NEXT PAGE

15. Refer to the pictograph below.

Capacity of Four Campgrounds

Camp Spiderweb	△ △ △ △
Camp Bear Cave	△ △ △ △ △ △
Camp Owl's Nest	△ △
Camp Fox's Den	△ △ △ △ △

△ = 100 campers

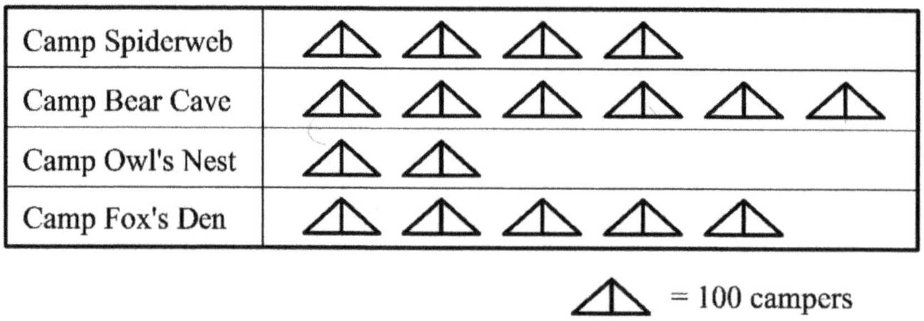

The graph above shows the capacity of four campgrounds. How many more campers can stay at Camp Bear Cave than at Camp Owl's Nest?

(A) 4
(B) 40
(C) 400
(D) 600

16. Use input/output table below to answer the question.

Input	Output
6	1
12	2
36	⊡
54	9

What is the value of ⊡?

(A) 3
(B) 6
(C) 7
(D) 8

CONTINUE TO THE NEXT PAGE

17. A bag of marbles has 5 green marbles, 4 blue marbles, 7 yellow marbles, and 6 red marbles. If a marble is drawn at random, what is the probability that it will be red?

(A) 1 out of 4
(B) 2 out of 22
(C) 3 out of 5
(D) 3 out of 11

18. Robyn wants to estimate the product 3.15 × 4.87. Which would give her the best estimate?

(A) 3 × 4
(B) 3 × 5
(C) 4 × 4
(D) 4 × 5

19. Wesley wants to use the distributive property to solve 12 × (9 + 16). Which expression would allow Wesley to solve?

(A) (12 × 9) + (12 × 16)
(B) (12 × 9) × (12 × 16)
(C) (12 + 9) + (12 + 16)
(D) (12 + 9) × (12 + 16)

20. Use the data table below.

Krista's Gymnastics Scores

Mat	5.9	6.8	7.2	6.9
Bar	8.9	9.2	9.5	8.5
Balance Beam	7.2	8.0	6.8	6.9
Rings	6.9	9.4	8.3	7.9

What is the range of this data?

(A) 3.5
(B) 3.6
(C) 7.2
(D) 9.5

CONTINUE TO THE NEXT PAGE

21. Use the number set below to answer the question.

$$\{4, 6, 8, 9, 10, ...\}$$

Which term best describes the numbers above?

(A) even numbers
(B) odd numbers
(C) composite numbers
(D) prime numbers

22. Milton buys a box of 36 pencils. The pencils are packaged in groups of 4. If g represents the number of groups in the box, which equation could be used to solve for how many groups are in the box?

(A) $4 + g = 36$
(B) $36 - 4 = g$
(C) $4 \div g = 36$
(D) $g = 36 \div 4$

23. Refer to the pentagon in the figure below.

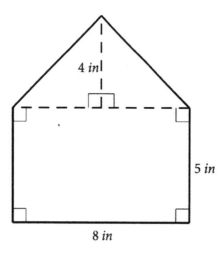

4 in

5 in

8 in

What is the area of the pentagon shown in the figure above?

(A) 40 in²
(B) 48 in²
(C) 56 in²
(D) 72 in²

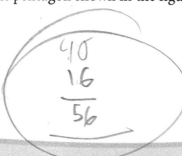

$$\begin{array}{r} 40 \\ 16 \\ \hline 56 \end{array}$$

CONTINUE TO THE NEXT PAGE

24. Which fraction is between 0.50 and 0.75?

(A) $\dfrac{5}{8}$

(B) $\dfrac{1}{3}$

(C) $\dfrac{1}{4}$

(D) $\dfrac{9}{10}$

25. Use the sequence below to answer the question.

$$3, 6, 12, 21, 33, \underline{\quad}$$

What number should replace the ____?

(A) 36
(B) 39
(C) 48
(D) 52

26. The square root of 40 is

(A) between 6 and 7
(B) between 7 and 8
(C) between 8 and 9
(D) between 9 and 10

27. A box contains red and blue cards. The probability of randomly choosing a red card is 5 out of 7. If there are 10 blue cards, then how many total cards are in the box?

(A) 10
(B) 25
(C) 35
(D) 40

CONTINUE TO THE NEXT PAGE

28. Use the coordinate grid below.

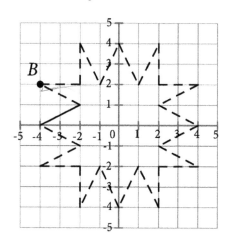

What are the coordinates of point *B*?

(A) $(2, -4)$

(B) $(-4, 2)$

(C) $(-4, -2)$

(D) $(-2, -4)$

29. Jesse had $6\frac{2}{3}$ feet of rope. He gave his friend $3\frac{5}{6}$ feet of that rope. How much rope does he have left?

(A) $1\frac{5}{6}$

(B) $2\frac{1}{3}$

(C) $2\frac{2}{3}$

(D) $2\frac{5}{6}$

$6\frac{4}{6}$ $5\frac{5}{6}$

30. What is the sum of 15 and the quotient of 35 and 7?

(A) 5

(B) 15

(C) 18

(D) 20

STOP

IF YOU HAVE TIME LEFT YOU MAY CHECK YOUR ANSWERS IN THIS SECTION ONLY

Essay

You will be given 30 minutes to plan and write an essay. The topic is printed on the next page. *Make sure that you write about this topic. Do NOT choose another topic.*

This essay gives you the chance to show your thinking and how well you can express your ideas. Do not worry about filling all of the space provided. The quality is more important than how much you write. You should write more than a brief paragraph, though.

A copy of this essay will be sent to the schools that you apply to. Make sure that you only write in the appropriate area on the answer sheet. Please print so that the admissions officers can understand what you wrote.

On the next page is the topic sheet. There is room on this sheet to make notes and collect your thoughts. The final essay should be written on the two lined sheets provided in the answer sheet, however. Make sure that you copy your topic at the top of the first lined page. Write only in blue or black ink. (Answer sheets are found at the beginning of this book and you can go to www.testprepworks.com/student/download to download additional copies.)

REMINDER: Please remember to write the topic on the top of the first lined page in your answer sheet.

> What is your favorite hobby? Why is it your favorite?

- Write only about this topic
- Only the lined sheets will be sent to schools
- Use only blue or black ink

Notes

_____

_____

_____

_____

_____

_____

_____

_____

_____

_____

_____

_____

_____

_____

_____

_____

_____

_____

_____

Answers for Practice Test 1

Verbal Reasoning Answers

Correct answer	Your answer	Put a checkmark here if you answered the question correctly
1. A		
2. D		
3. B		
4. A		
5. C		
6. B		
7. D		
8. C		
9. D		
10. C		
11. A		
12. A		
13. B		
14. D		
15. C		
16. B		
17. A		
18. B		
19. C		
20. A		
21. D		
22. A		
23. B		
24. C		
25. B		
26. D		
27. A		
28. C		
29. B		
30. A		
31. D		
32. C		
33. A		
34. B		
Total questions answered correctly: _____		

Interpreting Your Verbal Reasoning Score

On the ISEE, your raw score is the number of questions that you answered correctly on each section. Nothing is subtracted for the questions that you answered incorrectly.

Your raw score is then converted into a scaled score. This scaled score is then converted into a percentile score. Remember that it is the percentile score that schools are looking at. Your percentile score compares you just to other students in your grade.

Below is a chart that gives a very rough conversion between your raw score on the practice Verbal Reasoning section and a percentile score.

PLEASE NOTE – The purpose of this chart is to let you see how the scoring works, not to give you an accurate percentile score. You will need to complete the official practice test in *What to Expect on the ISEE*, available for download from ERB at www.erblearn.org, in order to get a more accurate percentile score.

Lower Level Verbal Reasoning

Applicants to Grade 5			
Percentile score	25th	50th	75th
Approximate raw score needed	19-20	22-23	27-28

Applicants to Grade 6			
Percentile score	25th	50th	75th
Approximate raw score needed	21-22	26-27	30-31

Quantitative Reasoning Answers

Correct answer	Your answer	Put a checkmark here if you answered the question correctly
1. A		
2. D		
3. C		
4. B		
5. B		
6. A		
7. D		
8. D		
9. B		
10. C		
11. A		
12. B		
13. D		
14. B		
15. C		
16. D		
17. C		
18. A		
19. B		
20. D		
21. D		
22. A		
23. A		
24. C		
25. C		
26. C		
27. B		
28. B		
29. D		
30. A		
31. C		
32. D		
33. B		
34. C		
35. A		
36. B		
37. A		
38. C		
Total questions answered correctly: _____		

Interpreting Your Quantitative Reasoning Score

On the ISEE, your raw score is the number of questions that you answered correctly on each section. Nothing is subtracted for the questions that you answered incorrectly.

Your raw score is then converted into a scaled score. This scaled score is then converted into a percentile score. Remember that it is the percentile score that schools are looking at. Your percentile score compares you just to other students in your grade.

Below is a chart that gives a very rough conversion between your raw score on the practice Quantitative Reasoning section and a percentile score.

PLEASE NOTE – The purpose of this chart is to let you see how the scoring works, not to give you an accurate percentile score. You will need to complete the official practice test in *What to Expect on the ISEE*, available for download from ERB at www.erblearn.org, in order to get a more accurate percentile score.

Lower Level Quantitative Reasoning

Applicants to Grade 5			
Percentile score	25th	50th	75th
Approximate raw score needed	17-18	21-22	27-28

Applicants to Grade 6			
Percentile score	25th	50th	75th
Approximate raw score needed	21-22	24-25	28-29

Reading Comprehension Answers

Correct answer	Your answer	Put a checkmark here if you answered the question correctly
1. C		
2. A		
3. B		
4. D		
5. B		
6. C		
7. A		
8. D		
9. B		
10. A		
11. C		
12. B		
13. D		
14. B		
15. A		
16. C		
17. D		
18. A		
19. B		
20. C		
21. A		
22. D		
23. C		
24. B		
25. A		
Total questions answered correctly: _____		

Interpreting Your Reading Comprehension Score

On the ISEE, your raw score is the number of questions that you answered correctly on each section. Nothing is subtracted for the questions that you answered incorrectly.

Your raw score is then converted into a scaled score. This scaled score is then converted into a percentile score. Remember that it is the percentile score that schools are looking at. Your percentile score compares you just to other students in your grade.

Below is a chart that gives a very rough conversion between your raw score on the practice Reading Comprehension section and a percentile score.

PLEASE NOTE – The purpose of this chart is to let you see how the scoring works, not to give you an accurate percentile score. You will need to complete the official practice test in *What to Expect on the ISEE*, available for download from ERB at www.erblearn.org, in order to get a more accurate percentile score.

Lower Level Reading Comprehension

Applicants to Grade 5			
Percentile score	25th	50th	75th
Approximate raw score needed	10-11	14-15	18-19

Applicants to Grade 6			
Percentile score	25th	50th	75th
Approximate raw score needed	12-13	16-17	20-21

Mathematics Achievement Answers

Correct answer	Your answer	Put a checkmark here if you answered the question correctly
1. B		
2. C		
3. A		
4. D		
5. C		
6. B		
7. A		
8. D		
9. B		
10. C		
11. D		
12. B		
13. A		
14. A		
15. C		
16. B		
17. D		
18. B		
19. A		
20. B		
21. C		
22. D		
23. C		
24. A		
25. C		
26. A		
27. C		
28. B		
29. D		
30. D		
Total questions answered correctly: _____		

Interpreting Your Mathematics Achievement Score

On the ISEE, your raw score is the number of questions that you answered correctly on each section. Nothing is subtracted for the questions that you answered incorrectly.

Your raw score is then converted into a scaled score. This scaled score is then converted into a percentile score. Remember that it is the percentile score that schools are looking at. Your percentile score compares you just to other students in your grade.

Below is a chart that gives a very rough conversion between your raw score on the practice Mathematics Achievement section and a percentile score.

PLEASE NOTE – The purpose of this chart is to let you see how the scoring works, not to give you an accurate percentile score. You will need to complete the official practice test in *What to Expect on the ISEE*, available for download from ERB at www.erblearn.org, in order to get a more accurate percentile score.

Lower Level Mathematics Achievement

Applicants to Grade 5			
Percentile score	25th	50th	75th
Approximate raw score needed	18-19	22-23	26-27

Applicants to Grade 6			
Percentile score	25th	50th	75th
Approximate raw score needed	21-22	25-26	27-28

Practice Test 2

Verbal Reasoning

34 questions

20 minutes

Part One- Synonyms

Directions: For each question, a word is given in capital letters. Select the answer choice that has the word that is closest in meaning to the word given in capital letters.

1. DISPLEASE:

   (A) collect
   (B) nudge
   (C) offend
   (D) suggest

2. MEND:

   (A) dread
   (B) pronounce
   (C) qualify
   (D) repair

3. ERRONEOUS:

   (A) broad
   (B) drab
   (C) peaceful
   (D) wrong

4. MODERATE:

   (A) bitter
   (B) modest
   (C) muscular
   (D) valiant

CONTINUE TO THE NEXT PAGE

5. DEFECTIVE:

   (A) broken
   (B) fluid
   (C) punctual
   (D) warily

6. SPECTACULAR:

   (A) amazing
   (B) nimble
   (C) reasonable
   (D) swollen

7. TURBULENT:

   (A) accepting
   (B) blank
   (C) choppy
   (D) entertaining

8. INFINITE:

   (A) defeated
   (B) immediate
   (C) popular
   (D) unlimited

9. SAGA:

   (A) award
   (B) product
   (C) story
   (D) victory

10. MAGNITUDE:

   (A) privilege
   (B) size
   (C) sympathy
   (D) triumph

CONTINUE TO THE NEXT PAGE

11. ENCLOSE:

   (A) contain
   (B) fuel
   (C) reserve
   (D) twirl

12. JUNCTION:

   (A) affection
   (B) fraction
   (C) habit
   (D) intersection

13. INCOMPLETE:

   (A) crooked
   (B) lively
   (C) precious
   (D) unfinished

14. PROSPEROUS:

   (A) civil
   (B) lonely
   (C) successful
   (D) united

15. COMPILE:

   (A) gather
   (B) kneel
   (C) provide
   (D) taste

16. EMBRACE:

   (A) discard
   (B) imply
   (C) welcome
   (D) writhe

CONTINUE TO THE NEXT PAGE

17. FAMISHED:

   (A) blistering
   (B) hungry
   (C) limber
   (D) renewed

Part Two- Sentence Completions

Directions: Choose the answer that best completes the meaning of the sentence.

18. It is truly ------- when the sun rises over the snow-capped Rocky Mountains and spills into the valley below.

   (A) agreeable
   (B) economical
   (C) private
   (D) splendid

19. Edgar Allan Poe's short stories are full of ------- details such as dark cemeteries, crumbling castles, and characters who return from the grave.

   (A) creepy
   (B) elegant
   (C) lazy
   (D) typical

20. Thomas Jefferson showed his -------- support of the explorers Meriwether Lewis and William Clark by providing money and supplies for their trip even when other people objected to the expense.

   (A) artificial
   (B) difficult
   (C) steadfast
   (D) vanishing

CONTINUE TO THE NEXT PAGE

21. Although many Americans were rural farmers before the Industrial Revolution, the increase in the number of urban factory jobs led many people to move to -------.

    (A) cities
    (B) houses
    (C) mountains
    (D) orchards

22. Compared to its relatives, such as the ferocious wild cougar, the average housecat is very -------.

    (A) appropriate
    (B) old-fashioned
    (C) skillful
    (D) tame

23. Harry proved that he was very ------- by showing up on time every day for a year.

    (A) abrupt
    (B) fearless
    (C) reliable
    (D) tragic

24. In cold climates like North Dakota, where the temperature is often well below zero in the winter, a backup heating system is --------.

    (A) invalid
    (B) recommended
    (C) salvaged
    (D) tedious

25. Although many comedians have a routine that is scripted and well-practiced, many others prefer to ----------.

    (A) assume
    (B) improvise
    (C) scurry
    (D) yield

CONTINUE TO THE NEXT PAGE

26. Pine trees are often the only trees living high on mountains with harsh conditions because they are able to ------- high winds and extreme temperatures that kill other trees.

   (A) advance
   (B) concentrate
   (C) perform
   (D) withstand

27. Lindsey Vonn showed real --------- when she recovered from numerous injuries and continued to compete in skiing events.

   (A) courage
   (B) fatigue
   (C) observation
   (D) respect

28. Because mosquitoes can infect people with the disease malaria, they are a real ------- to public health in some countries.

   (A) menace
   (B) promotion
   (C) observation
   (D) triumph

29. Before Ernest Hemingway, most American writers used very descriptive language, but Ernest Hemingway introduced -------.

   (A) the idea of the novel
   (B) writing with very little detail
   (C) stories about travelling
   (D) a new system of printing

30. Although it is hard to determine the exact cause of the fire, -------.

   (A) it was hard to put out
   (B) it did not burn for long
   (C) many people have suggested possible sources
   (D) it may be repeated

CONTINUE TO THE NEXT PAGE

31. Despite his reputation for being a wonderful public speaker, Winston Churchill actually -------.

   (A) had to overcome a speech impediment
   (B) was a leader
   (C) received awards for public speaking
   (D) enjoyed movies

32. Since the shipment did not arrive at the right time, the grocery store -------.

   (A) sold green beans
   (B) bought more cans of chicken soup
   (C) opened early
   (D) had nobody available to unload it

33. Although most violins have only four strings, they -------.

   (A) can only play a few notes
   (B) are one of the earliest instruments
   (C) can be used to play many different notes
   (D) last a long time

34. Despite the general trend of warmer winters, this winter was ---------.

   (A) a leap year
   (B) the coldest on record
   (C) the warmest in many years
   (D) worth celebrating

STOP

IF YOU HAVE TIME LEFT YOU MAY CHECK YOUR ANSWERS IN THIS SECTION ONLY

Quantitative Reasoning

38 questions

35 minutes

Directions: Each of the following math questions has four possible answers after it. Choose the correct answer for the question.

1. Use the figures shown below.

   What fraction of the figures above are ovals?

   (A) $\dfrac{3}{10}$

   (B) $\dfrac{1}{3}$

   (C) $\dfrac{3}{8}$

   (D) $\dfrac{1}{2}$

2. Jerome has a box of 36 cookies. He wants to distribute them equally among 12 people. Which operation should he do in order to figure out how many cookies each person should get?

   (A) $36 + 12$
   (B) $36 - 12$
   (C) 36×12
   (D) $36 \div 12$

CONTINUE TO THE NEXT PAGE

3. Allen's baseball team won more than 7 games but less than 12 games. They also won more than 4 games but less than 9 games. How many games did Allen's team win?

(A) 7
(B) 8
(C) 9
(D) 10

4. Which answer choice correctly illustrates the commutative property?

(A) $3(2 + 5) = (3 \times 2) + (3 \times 5)$
(B) $(3 + 2) + 5 = 3 + (2 + 5)$
(C) $3 + 2 + 5 = 2 + 5 + 3$
(D) $3 + 2 \times 5 = 2 + 3 \times 5$

5. Ollie and Marcos were running at the same speed. It took Ollie 40 minutes to run 5 miles. How long did it take Marcos to run 6 miles?

(A) 36 minutes
(B) 40 minutes
(C) 44 minutes
(D) 48 minutes

6. Which of the following represents two thousand four hundred six?

(A) 2,406
(B) 2,460
(C) 2,466
(D) 2,640

CONTINUE TO THE NEXT PAGE

7. The perimeter of the rectangle below is 34 cm. The length of the rectangle is shown.

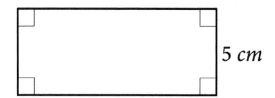

5 *cm*

What is the width of the rectangle?

(A) 10 cm
(B) 12 cm
(C) 24 cm
(D) 29 cm

8. Use the figure below to answer the question

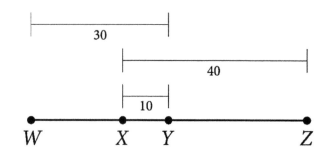

What is the length of *WZ*?

(A) 40
(B) 50
(C) 60
(D) 80

CONTINUE TO THE NEXT PAGE

9. To answer the question, use the equations below.

$$9 - m = 5$$
$$12 - n = 5$$

What is the value of $n - m$?

(A) 3
(B) 4
(C) 5
(D) 7

10. Which fraction has the greatest value?

(A) $\dfrac{4}{9}$

(B) $\dfrac{5}{11}$

(C) $\dfrac{9}{19}$

(D) $\dfrac{11}{21}$

11. Use the number line below to answer the question.

What number is the arrow above pointing to?

(A) $2\dfrac{1}{2}$

(B) $2\dfrac{2}{3}$

(C) $2\dfrac{5}{6}$

(D) $2\dfrac{9}{10}$

CONTINUE TO THE NEXT PAGE

12. Use the Venn Diagram below to answer the question.

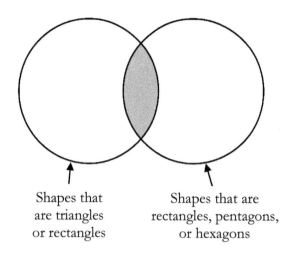

Shapes that are triangles or rectangles

Shapes that are rectangles, pentagons, or hexagons

Which shape would belong in the shaded portion of the Venn Diagram?

(A) A purple triangle
(B) A gray rectangle
(C) A pink pentagon
(D) A green hexagon

13. The number 372 can be divided by both 3 and 4 with no remainder left over. Which of the following numbers can it also be divided by and leave no remainder?

(A) 7
(B) 8
(C) 9
(D) 12

14. Wendell has red, green, and blue marbles in a bag. He has twice as many green marbles as red marbles and three times as many blue marbles than red marbles. If he has 18 total marbles, how many of them are green?

(A) 3
(B) 4
(C) 6
(D) 12

CONTINUE TO THE NEXT PAGE

15. Use the coordinate grid to answer the question.

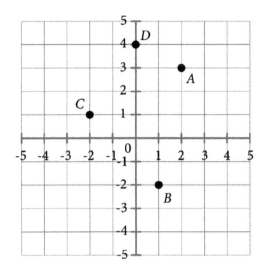

What are the coordinates of point *B*?

(A) $(-2, 1)$
(B) $(-1, 2)$
(C) $(1, -2)$
(D) $(-1, -2)$

16. Use the pattern below to answer the question.

$$3, 5, 8, 12, \_\_, 23$$

Which number should replace the _____?

(A) 16
(B) 17
(C) 18
(D) 20

17. Which of the following does not equal 100?

(A) $0.01 \times 10,000$
(B) $0.1 \times 1,000$
(C) 10×10
(D) $10 \times 10 \times 10$

CONTINUE TO THE NEXT PAGE

18. Use the x-y chart below to answer the question.

Input x	Output y
2	5
4	9
10	21
12	25
24	49

Which rule works for this function?

(A) $y = x + 3$
(B) $y = 3x - 1$
(C) $y = 2x + 1$
(D) $y = x + 5$

19. If $20 = 4x + 4$, then what is the value of x?

(A) 4
(B) 5
(C) 6
(D) 7

CONTINUE TO THE NEXT PAGE

20. Ann surveyed her classmates about their favorite activities. The results of her survey are shown below.

If 24 students preferred reading, how many students preferred playing video games?

(A) 24
(B) 48
(C) 72
(D) 96

21. On a certain test, two students each scored an 85, one student scored a 90, and one student scored a 100. What is the mean score of all the students?

(A) 85

(B) 90

(C) $91\frac{2}{3}$

(D) 95

22. Tonya went to the grocery store and bought two gallons of milk that cost $4 each and a loaf of bread (b). If her total bill (without tax) was $11, then which equation would allow Tonya to figure out how much the loaf of bread cost?

(A) $4 + b = 11$
(B) $4 + 2b = 11$
(C) $2(4) + b = 11$
(D) $2(4) + 2b = 11$

CONTINUE TO THE NEXT PAGE

23. Which figure has an infinite number of lines of symmetry?

(A)

(B)

(C)

(D)

24. Naomi is building a garden that has a 2-foot border around it, as shown below.

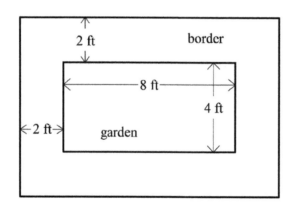

What is the area of the land covered just by the border (and not by the garden)?

(A) 64 sq. ft.
(B) 72 sq. ft.
(C) 84 sq. ft.
(D) 96 sq. ft.

CONTINUE TO THE NEXT PAGE

25. Mr. Richardson wrote the names of all of his students on small balls and put them in a jar. If he randomly chooses a name, the probability that the name will belong to a girl is 3 out of 5. If there are 25 students in his class, how many of them are boys?

(A) 8
(B) 10
(C) 15
(D) 20

26. In the figure below, the volume of the smaller shaded cube is 1 cm³.

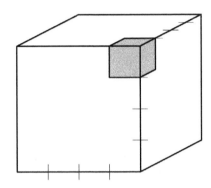

What is the volume of the larger cube?

(A) 6 cm³
(B) 36 cm³
(C) 64 cm³
(D) 72 cm³

CONTINUE TO THE NEXT PAGE

27. Use the figure below to answer the question.

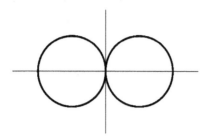

How many lines of symmetry does the figure above have?

(A) 1
(B) 2
(C) 3
(D) 4

28. Julia has two bottles of mustard, each of which hold 12 ounces when full. One bottle is half full and the other bottle is two-thirds full. If Julia combines the contents of both bottles, how many ounces of mustard will she have?

(A) 6 ounces
(B) 8 ounces
(C) 12 ounces
(D) 14 ounces

29. Maria is building a scale model of a ship. The scale is that 10 feet on the actual ship is equal to 1.4 inches on the model. If the actual ship is 35 feet long, then how many inches long should Maria's model be?

(A) 4.9 inches
(B) 5.2 inches
(C) 6.5 inches
(D) 14.0 inches

CONTINUE TO THE NEXT PAGE

30. Guy knows that 3 more than 4 times a number is equal to 6 less than that number. Which equation could he use to figure out the number? Let v represent the number.

(A) $3 + (4 \times v) = 6 - v$
(B) $3 \times (4 + v) = 6 - v$
(C) $3 + (4 \times v) = v - 6$
(D) $3 \times (4 + v) = v - 6$

31. Use the hexagon below.

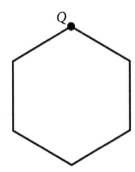

If lines are drawn connecting point Q to each of the other vertices, how many triangular sections would be created?

(A) 3
(B) 4
(C) 5
(D) 6

32. Use the following equation to answer the question.

$$m = \frac{74 \times 657}{25}$$

Which is a reasonable estimate for the value of m?

(A) between 1900 and 2000
(B) between 2000 and 2400
(C) between 2400 and 3000
(D) between 3000 and 3500

CONTINUE TO THE NEXT PAGE

33. There are red, green, yellow, and blue t-shirts in a box. The probability of randomly drawing a green t-shirt is 3 out of 10. Which could be the combination of t-shirts in the box?

    (A) 3 green t-shirts and 10 others
    (B) 6 green t-shirts and 20 others
    (C) 9 green t-shirts and 18 others
    (D) 12 green t-shirts and 28 others

34. The average of *A* and *B* is 14. If *A* is equal to 6, then what is *B* equal to?

    (A) 10
    (B) 14
    (C) 22
    (D) 24

35. Use the figure below to answer the question.

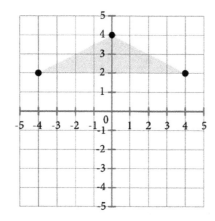

    What is the area of the shaded region?

    (A) 8
    (B) 10
    (C) 12
    (D) 16

CONTINUE TO THE NEXT PAGE

36. June combined $\frac{2}{3}$ cup of apple juice and $\frac{1}{4}$ cup of cranberry juice. How much juice did she have in total?

(A) $\frac{11}{12}$ cup

(B) $1\frac{1}{3}$ cups

(C) $1\frac{3}{5}$ cups

(D) $1\frac{11}{12}$ cups

37. Larry draws the following points on a coordinate graph: $(2, 4), (4, 7), (6, 4)$ and $(4, 1)$. If he connects these points, what kind of shape would be formed?

(A) rhombus
(B) square
(C) trapezoid
(D) right triangle

38. Which fraction has the greatest value?

(A) $\frac{5}{12}$

(B) $\frac{7}{15}$

(C) $\frac{10}{19}$

(D) $\frac{10}{21}$

STOP

IF YOU HAVE TIME LEFT YOU MAY CHECK YOUR ANSWERS IN THIS SECTION ONLY

Reading Comprehension

Directions: The reading comprehension section has five passages. Each passage has five questions after it. For each question, choose the answer that best reflects what is either implied or stated in the passage.

Questions #1-5

1   Gardens bursting with color and scent throughout the growing season are delightful
2   and not as difficult to achieve as one might think. The key is to include both perennials
3   and annuals, and to place them strategically throughout the garden plot.
4   Perennials are plants that will come back for many growing seasons. The top
5   portion of the plant seems to die in winter, but the root or bulb is still very much alive
6   under the soil. Some popular examples of perennials are asters, peonies, alstromeria,
7   lavender, and of course, roses. Perennials can be planted strategically so that one's garden
8   will be in bloom throughout spring, summer, and fall.
9   For those who want a more "hands on" approach to gardening, annuals are a good
10 choice, either in addition to or instead of perennials. Annuals are very much what their
11 name implies; that is, their life cycle from seed to flower to seed happens within one
12 growing season, or one year.
13   Once the perennials are planted in the garden, they will continue to bloom every
14 spring, summer and fall, depending on the blooming season of the individual plants.
15 Annuals, however, will have to be planted either from seed in spring or as a fully-grown
16 plant from a nursery.
17   The beauty of including both perennials and annuals in a garden is that one can
18 count on the perennials to be there year after year, and at the same time, it's possible to
19 spice things up with a variety of different annuals each spring.

CONTINUE TO THE NEXT PAGE

1. Which statement best captures the main idea of this passage?

   (A) A skilled gardener only needs perennials.
   (B) Perennials may appear to die but the roots live on underground.
   (C) Annuals must be grown from seed.
   (D) A mixture of annuals and perennials produces an attractive garden.

2. The author implies which of the following about annual plants?

   (A) They must be replanted every spring.
   (B) They regrow each spring without maintenance.
   (C) Roses are an example of an annual plant.
   (D) They require less work than perennial plants.

3. Which of the following could be inferred from the passage about perennials?

   (A) It is harder to find attractive perennials.
   (B) Different perennials bloom at different times of year.
   (C) Perennials are more colorful than annuals.
   (D) Perennials are usually purchased from a nursery.

4. The purpose of the last paragraph (lines 17-19) is to

   (A) summarize the advantages and disadvantages of annual plants.
   (B) create a sense of excitement for the reader.
   (C) describe why annuals and perennials are important.
   (D) offer a contradictory opinion.

5. In the last sentence (lines 17-19) the phrase "spice things up" most nearly means to

   (A) add spices.
   (B) provide further information.
   (C) encourage different types of plantings.
   (D) make something more interesting.

CONTINUE TO THE NEXT PAGE

1   During the time of westward expansion in the United States, many wagon trains
2 moved across the prairie from the East Coast toward Oregon and California. It was a
3 dangerous journey for people to undertake, and at times had fatal results. Such was the
4 case for the Donner Party.

5   The Donner Party was a group of 87 Americans heading to California. The party
6 included the families of George Donner and James Reed. They arrived in Independence,
7 Missouri, on May 10, 1846, to begin their westward journey. Two days later, they left for
8 California. While still in Missouri, the Donner Party joined a large wagon train that they
9 would follow until they got to Wyoming.

10   On July 19, 1846, the Donner Party decided to take a shortcut known as Hastings
11 Cutoff. They separated from the main wagon train. This would turn out to be a decision
12 with tragic consequences for them. The shortcut did not work and they wound up three
13 weeks behind schedule on their trip. When they reached the Sierra Nevada, they got
14 caught in a snowstorm. It blocked their passage and there was no way for them to reach
15 California before the spring of 1847.

16   The Donner Party was in quite a bit of trouble at this point. Supplies and morale
17 were both low. They set up two camps at Donner Lake that were six miles apart. The
18 storms of the west had trapped this party in a dangerous region of the country. They
19 were in unsettled land, unable to hunt or gather food.

20   The emigrants slaughtered their oxen, but there was not enough meat to feed that
21 many people for long. Fifteen men tried to use snowshoes to get to Sutter's Fort, which
22 was about 100 miles away. Seven people out of the fifteen died trying to reach California.
23 The eight surviving snowshoers reached California on January 19, 1847, six months after
24 the Donner Party took their ill-fated shortcut.

25   Four different rescue trips were necessary in order to bring the surviving members
26 of the Donner Party to safety. Each time a new team of rescuers arrived, they found the
27 survivors in worse condition. The last member of the Donner Party arrived at Sutter's
28 Fort on April 29th, 1847.

CONTINUE TO THE NEXT PAGE

6. This passage was probably written in order to

   (A) explain different routes to California.
   (B) relate a tragic story of one group.
   (C) discuss the dangerous conditions in winter.
   (D) describe the Donner family.

7. According to the passage, what primarily led to the tragedy of the Donner Party?

   (A) They decided to eat their oxen.
   (B) They set up two camps at Donner Lake.
   (C) The search parties did not act quickly enough.
   (D) They attempted to take a shortcut through Hastings Pass.

8. In line 19 the word "unsettled" most nearly means

   (A) not inhabited.
   (B) disturbed.
   (C) missing.
   (D) mountainous.

9. In the second paragraph (lines 5-9) the author implies that

   (A) Wyoming was a long distance from Missouri.
   (B) many wagon trains failed to make the journey west.
   (C) more than one wagon train travelled through Missouri.
   (D) George Donner's family was larger than James Reed's family.

10. Which of the following questions could be answered with information from the passage?

   (A) Where were the Donners originally from?
   (B) When did the Donner Party arrive in Independence, Missouri?
   (C) How many of the Donner Party survived?
   (D) What was the original planned route for the Donner Party?

CONTINUE TO THE NEXT PAGE

1   One summer my grandmother came to visit and brought along her father. My
2 great-grandfather was a kind man with a hearty laugh. He had a white, tickly moustache
3 that he wiggled at me while he rolled his eyes. He always had a mint for me in his pocket
4 as well. I didn't like mints, but he seemed so excited to offer the candy to me that I could
5 not refuse. I would unwind the plastic wrapper as slowly as possible and delicately pick
6 off stray pieces of fuzz left over from his pocket. This extended routine seemed to satisfy
7 him and I could often be spared actually putting the mint in my mouth.

8   On a hot afternoon, my grandmother decided that we should take a ride over to a
9 local park near the river to cool down. She carefully packed everything that we would
10 need in her bag. There was a bottle of sunscreen, water bottles, and hats for everyone. I
11 fussed over putting my sandals on so she carried me out to the car and put the bag beside
12 me. She went back for my sandals, came back to the car, put my shoes on top of the car,
13 and then leaned in to help my great-grandfather with his seatbelt. We arrived at the park
14 and realized that there were no sandals to be found. My great-grandfather just wiggled
15 his white moustache at me and said "It's OK. We will just walk slowly for Melanie's little
16 feet and great-grandpa's old heart."

CONTINUE TO THE NEXT PAGE

11. The primary purpose of this passage is to

    (A)   describe an experience that the author had.

    (B)   explain the importance of parks.

    (C)   provide details about what to bring to the park.

    (D)   criticize the author's grandmother.

12. In line 6 the word "extended" is closest in meaning to

    (A)   limited.

    (B)   delicate.

    (C)   deliberately annoying.

    (D)   longer than necessary.

13. It can be inferred that the author's sandals

    (A)   were never packed.

    (B)   had fallen off the top of the car and been left behind.

    (C)   were her favorite shoes.

    (D)   were later found.

14. Which word best describes the author's great-grandfather in the passage?

    (A)   forgetful

    (B)   disinterested

    (C)   kind

    (D)   energetic

15. Which of the following questions could be answered with information from the passage?

    (A)   How old was the author's great-grandfather?

    (B)   In what direction did they drive to get to the park?

    (C)   Did the author have any siblings?

    (D)   Did the author like mints?

CONTINUE TO THE NEXT PAGE

1   A dinner salad is a healthy and delicious accompaniment to any entrée. It is also a
2 simple way to impress guests or help out your family. By following these steps, you can
3 become an expert salad maker.

4   Always begin your dinner salad with greens. This can mean lettuce, like iceberg,
5 romaine, or Bibb, but there are other greens, too, like spinach and arugula. You can even
6 mix different greens together for variety. Some grocery stores sell bags of pre-washed
7 mixed greens for salads. If you wash and chop your own greens, be sure to pat them dry.

8   I like to add vegetables next. The variety of raw vegetables is almost endless –
9 carrots, peppers, onions, cucumbers – you name it. All raw vegetables need to be
10 scrubbed or peeled and then chopped into small pieces. There are also cooked or
11 marinated vegetables that are great on salads, like beets, peppers, or garbanzo beans
12 (which are really a legume, not a vegetable). Not only will vegetables add health benefits
13 to your salad, but they also add color.

14   The third ingredient in any good salad is something that adds crunch. That usually
15 means nuts or croutons. Many different nuts, like walnuts, pecans, or almonds, can be
16 toasted or crushed and sprinkled over the salad. I also put sunflower seeds in this
17 category, because they give a salad a salty crunch. Croutons are small toasted bits of
18 bread that come in a variety of seasonings. A salad just needs a little of this ingredient to
19 add texture.

20   Finally, top the salad with cheese or dressing for flavor. Different cheeses
21 complement different styles. For example, a Mexican salad would taste great with
22 cheddar and Greek salads usually use feta. If you add the dressing yourself, remember:
23 less is more. If your guests like the flavor, they can add more themselves.

24   Have fun experimenting with different ingredients and combinations. You can
25 even look through cookbooks or online recipes for inspiration. Be sure to use kitchen
26 safety, especially when cutting, and clean up after yourself. Your whole family will
27 benefit from your newfound talent!

CONTINUE TO THE NEXT PAGE

16. The primary purpose of this passage is to describe

   (A) what dressing to use on various salads.
   (B) how to make a good salad.
   (C) the importance of vegetables in your diet.
   (D) the difference between vegetables and legumes.

17. The tone of the passage can best be described as

   (A) bored.
   (B) excited.
   (C) informative.
   (D) mournful.

18. The function of the third paragraph (lines 8-13) is to

   (A) introduce a new viewpoint.
   (B) summarize an approach.
   (C) create a sense of suspense.
   (D) provide details for a step in a process.

19. What does the author imply about salad dressing?

   (A) It is necessary for making a good salad.
   (B) The type used depends on how far ahead the salad is prepared.
   (C) It is best when bought in a bottle.
   (D) A little bit goes a long way.

20. In line 12 the word "legume" most likely describes

   (A) a type of plant.
   (B) a meat product.
   (C) an ingredient that adds crunch.
   (D) a vegetable.

CONTINUE TO THE NEXT PAGE

1   Paul Revere is a famous figure in early American History. His famous cry, "The
2 British are coming!" is now the stuff of legends, lore, and poetry. But, what do we know
3 about this brave man?

4   Right before his famous ride, there was a stirring of trouble between the colonies
5 and Britain. At the time, America did not exist as an independent country. Rather, the
6 area that was to become the United States was a group of colonies ruled by the British.
7 The thirteen colonies were preparing to go to war with Britain. In 1775, the British army
8 was planning to invade Massachusetts. The colonists needed to be warned when the
9 British arrived. But how could they be informed in time?

10   Paul Revere was a member of an organization called "The Sons of Liberty." This
11 group existed in order to fight British oppression. Revere was asked to ride from Boston,
12 MA, to Concord, MA, to warn the colonists that the British were going to march on
13 Lexington.

14   Revere and Robert Newman, another member of the "Sons of Liberty", arranged a
15 signal plan. Newman would climb to the top of the Old North Church in Boston while
16 Revere waited across the river. If the British invaded by land, Newman would hang one
17 lantern. If they invaded by sea, Newman would hang two lanterns. When it became
18 clear that the British were invading by sea, Newman hung two lanterns in the church
19 tower.

20   Revere, and other riders, sent word to houses all over Massachusetts warning
21 colonists that the British were approaching by sea. Revere and William Dawes then
22 headed for Concord to prepare for battle with the British. They were arrested. Dawes
23 escaped and Revere was questioned at gunpoint. He was eventually freed and went on
24 to fight in the American Revolution.

25   Still, Paul Revere is best remembered for his midnight ride, which was made famous
26 by a poem written by Henry Wadsworth Longfellow. The poem is not historically
27 accurate because it states that Revere was a lone rider. However, the poem helped make
28 Paul Revere into a famous folk legend and today it is studied by schoolchildren across
29 America.

CONTINUE TO THE NEXT PAGE

21. The main idea of this passage is best expressed by which statement?

    (A) The "Sons of Liberty" were responsible for starting the American Revolution.
    (B) Robert Newman is not well-known.
    (C) Paul Revere is most famous for warning colonists that the British were invading.
    (D) Early American history is complex.

22. As used in line 6 the word "colonies" refers to

    (A) areas ruled by another country.
    (B) independent groups of people.
    (C) cruel leaders.
    (D) undiscovered lands.

23. According to the passage, Paul Revere

    (A) was a British soldier.
    (B) was not the only rider who looked for Robert Newman's lantern.
    (C) rode alone.
    (D) did not fight in the American Revolution.

24. The passage implies that Henry Wadsworth Longfellow believed that

    (A) the American Revolution would have been lost without Paul Revere.
    (B) Robert Newman was not worthy of being put into a poem.
    (C) it was better that the British came by sea rather than by land.
    (D) the tale of Paul Revere riding through the night made a great story.

25. Which question can be answered with information from the passage?

    (A) Who was the British commander?
    (B) Who won the battle in Lexington?
    (C) How did Paul Revere know that the British were coming by sea?
    (D) What year did the American Revolution end?

STOP

IF YOU HAVE TIME LEFT YOU MAY CHECK YOUR ANSWERS IN THIS SECTION ONLY

Mathematics Achievement

30 minutes

30 questions

Directions: Each of the following math questions has four possible answers after it. Choose the correct answer for the question.

1. Which number can be divided by 4 without leaving a remainder?

    (A) 312
    (B) 414
    (C) 453
    (D) 502

2. Use the rectangle below.

    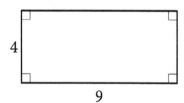

    What is the perimeter of the rectangle above? $(P = 2l + 2w)$

    (A) 13
    (B) 24
    (C) 26
    (D) 36

CONTINUE TO THE NEXT PAGE

3. What is the result of $800 - 67$?

   (A) 727
   (B) 733
   (C) 737
   (D) 743

4. Which is the name of a shape that always has four sides of all the same length?

   (A) rectangle
   (B) right triangle
   (C) trapezoid
   (D) rhombus

5. Peggy had a box with 36 pencils in it. She gave 15 pencils to her teacher and 6 pencils to a friend. How many pencils did she have left in her box?

   (A) 14
   (B) 15
   (C) 18
   (D) 20

6. Which is the written form for 340,023?

   (A) three hundred four thousand twenty-three
   (B) three hundred four thousand two hundred three
   (C) three hundred forty thousand twenty-three
   (D) three hundred forty thousand three

7. Use the number line below.

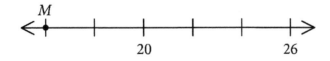

What is the value of point M?

   (A) 16
   (B) 18
   (C) 19
   (D) 22

CONTINUE TO THE NEXT PAGE

8. Eula had $50. She bought four coloring books for $3 each, one box of markers that cost $5, and one box of colored pencils that cost $7. How much money did she have left?

(A) $20
(B) $24
(C) $26
(D) $35

9. Use the equation below.

$$(\blacksquare + 4) \times 3 = 15$$

What number should replace the $\blacksquare$ in order to make the equation true?

(A) 1
(B) 2
(C) 3
(D) 5

10. Which equation correctly demonstrates the distributive property?

(A) $(3 + 4) + 5 = 3 + (4 + 5)$
(B) $3 + 4 + 5 = 3 + 5 + 4$
(C) $3(4 + 5) = (3 \times 4) \times (4 \times 5)$
(D) $3(4 + 5) = (3 \times 4) + (3 \times 5)$

11. Ray wants to estimate the product 3.12×5.9. Which would give him the best estimate?

(A) 3×5
(B) 3×6
(C) 4×5
(D) 4×6

12. Which decimal is equivalent to $\dfrac{23}{100}$?

(A) 0.00023
(B) 0.0023
(C) 0.023
(D) 0.23

CONTINUE TO THE NEXT PAGE

13. Use the equation below.

$$B \times B \times B \times B = B + B + B$$

What value of B would make the equation true?

(A) 0
(B) 1
(C) 2
(D) 3

14. In a box of crackers, there are 6 individual packages. Each package contains 18 crackers. Which equation could be used to figure out how many total crackers (c) are in a box?

(A) $6 + 18 = c$
(B) $18 \div 6 = c$
(C) $18 \times 6 = c$
(D) $18 - 6 = c$

15. An input/output machine is used to create numbers. The same operation is performed to each input number in order to create an output number.

Input	Output
3	10
5	16
10	31
11	34
?	40

Which input would create an output of 40?

(A) 12
(B) 13
(C) 15
(D) 16

CONTINUE TO THE NEXT PAGE

16. Which fraction is equivalent to $\frac{5}{6}$?

(A) $\dfrac{25}{30}$

(B) $\dfrac{25}{36}$

(C) $\dfrac{30}{42}$

(D) $\dfrac{30}{48}$

17. Charlie has a box with red, green, white, and blue chips in it. There are 5 red chips, 10 blue chips, 6 white chips, and 9 green chips. If he randomly selects a chip, which color chip has a 3 in 10 chance of being selected?

(A) red
(B) blue
(C) white
(D) green

18. Use the figure below to answer the question.

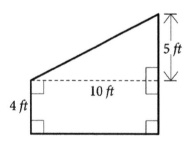

What is the area of the above shape?

(A) 45 ft²
(B) 60 ft²
(C) 65 ft²
(D) 90 ft²

CONTINUE TO THE NEXT PAGE

19. Which fraction is between $\frac{1}{2}$ and $\frac{7}{9}$?

(A) $\frac{2}{5}$

(B) $\frac{3}{5}$

(C) $\frac{6}{13}$

(D) $\frac{7}{15}$

20. Use the number set below to answer the question.

$\{2, 4, 6, 8, ...\}$

Which term best describes the numbers above?

(A) prime numbers
(B) consecutive numbers
(C) odd numbers
(D) even numbers

21. Use the pattern below to answer the question.

$3, 4, 6, 9, 13, 18, \underline{\quad}$

If the same pattern continues, what would be the next number in the sequence?

(A) 24
(B) 25
(C) 26
(D) 28

CONTINUE TO THE NEXT PAGE

22. The graph below shows the number of students in attendance at East Ridge High School each day for a week.

Number of Students in Attendance

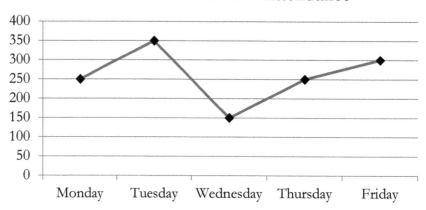

How many more students were in attendance on Monday than on Wednesday?

(A) 2
(B) 50
(C) 100
(D) 150

23. What is the sum of 10 and the product of 6 and 8?

(A) 24
(B) 58
(C) 68
(D) 480

24. What is the sum of $3\frac{2}{5} + 4\frac{1}{2}$?

(A) 7.3
(B) 7.4
(C) 7.6
(D) 7.9

CONTINUE TO THE NEXT PAGE

25. Joshua made a table of how many students stayed after school for four weeks. His data is shown in the table below.

Number of students who stayed afterschool

	Monday	Tuesday	Wednesday	Thursday	Friday
Week 1	43	46	32	43	50
Week 2	32	50	43	33	36
Week 3	43	40	33	40	43
Week 4	50	32	49	43	51

What is the mode of this data?

(A) 32
(B) 36
(C) 43
(D) 50

26. The cards in a deck are shown below.

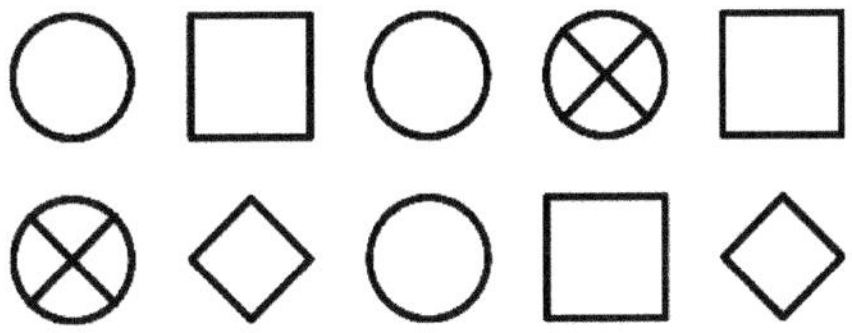

If a card is drawn at random, what is the chance that the card will NOT

have  on it?

(A) $\dfrac{1}{10}$

(B) $\dfrac{1}{5}$

(C) $\dfrac{2}{5}$

(D) $\dfrac{4}{5}$

CONTINUE TO THE NEXT PAGE

27. Use the coordinate grid below.

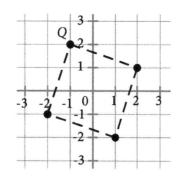

What are the coordinates of point Q?

(A) $(-1, 2)$
(B) $(1, -2)$
(C) $(-2, 1)$
(D) $(2, -1)$

28. Use the pictograph below to answer the question.

Number of pencils sold in one day

Larry's School Supplies	
Marco's Stationery	
Sally's Emporium	

If Larry's School Supplies sold 90 pencils, then how many pencils did Sally's Emporium sell?

(A) 4
(B) 80
(C) 85
(D) 90

CONTINUE TO THE NEXT PAGE

29. The figure below was created by stacking smaller one-inch cubes.

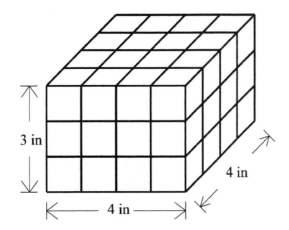

How many one-inch cubes were used to create the larger prism?

(A) 32
(B) 44
(C) 48
(D) 56

30. Lorraine has read 36 pages from a 72-page long report. What percent of the report has she read?

(A) 0%
(B) 25%
(C) 50%
(D) 75%

STOP

IF YOU HAVE TIME LEFT YOU MAY CHECK YOUR ANSWERS IN THIS SECTION ONLY

Essay

You will be given 30 minutes to plan and write an essay. The topic is printed on the next page. *Make sure that you write about this topic. Do NOT choose another topic.*

This essay gives you the chance to show your thinking and how well you can express your ideas. Do not worry about filling all of the space provided. The quality is more important than how much you write. You should write more than a brief paragraph, though.

A copy of this essay will be sent to the schools that you apply to. Make sure that you only write in the appropriate area on the answer sheet. Please print so that the admissions officers can understand what you wrote.

On the next page is the topic sheet. There is room on this sheet to make notes and collect your thoughts. The final essay should be written on the two lined sheets provided in the answer sheet, however. Make sure that you copy your topic at the top of the first lined page. Write only in blue or black ink. (Answer sheets are found at the beginning of this book and you can go to www.testprepworks.com/student/download to download additional copies.)

REMINDER: Please remember to write the topic on the top of the first lined page in your answer sheet.

What job would you like to do when you grow up?
Why would you like to do this job?

- Write only about this topic
- Only the lined sheets will be sent to schools
- Use only blue or black ink

Notes

_____
_____
_____
_____
_____
_____
_____
_____
_____
_____
_____
_____
_____
_____
_____
_____
_____
_____
_____
_____
_____

Answers for Practice Test 2

Verbal Reasoning Answers

Correct answer	Your answer	Put a checkmark here if you answered the question correctly
1. C		
2. D		
3. D		
4. B		
5. A		
6. A		
7. C		
8. D		
9. C		
10. B		
11. A		
12. D		
13. D		
14. C		
15. A		
16. C		
17. B		
18. D		
19. A		
20. C		
21. A		
22. D		
23. C		
24. B		
25. B		
26. D		
27. A		
28. A		
29. B		
30. C		
31. A		
32. D		
33. C		
34. B		
Total questions answered correctly: _____		

Interpreting Your Verbal Reasoning Score

On the ISEE, your raw score is the number of questions that you answered correctly on each section. Nothing is subtracted for the questions that you answered incorrectly.

Your raw score is then converted into a scaled score. This scaled score is then converted into a percentile score. Remember that it is the percentile score that schools are looking at. Your percentile score compares you just to other students in your grade.

Below is a chart that gives a very rough conversion between your raw score on the practice Verbal Reasoning section and a percentile score.

PLEASE NOTE – The purpose of this chart is to let you see how the scoring works, not to give you an accurate percentile score. You will need to complete the official practice test in *What to Expect on the ISEE*, available for download from ERB at www.erblearn.org, in order to get a more accurate percentile score.

Lower Level Verbal Reasoning

Applicants to Grade 5			
Percentile score	25th	50th	75th
Approximate raw score needed	19-20	22-23	27-28

Applicants to Grade 6			
Percentile score	25th	50th	75th
Approximate raw score needed	21-22	26-27	30-31

Quantitative Reasoning Answers

Correct answer	Your answer	Put a checkmark here if you answered the question correctly
1. A		
2. D		
3. B		
4. C		
5. D		
6. A		
7. B		
8. C		
9. A		
10. D		
11. C		
12. B		
13. D		
14. C		
15. C		
16. B		
17. D		
18. C		
19. A		
20. D		
21. B		
22. C		
23. D		
24. A		
25. B		
26. C		
27. B		
28. D		
29. A		
30. C		
31. B		
32. A		
33. D		
34. C		
35. A		
36. A		
37. A		
38. C		
Total questions answered correctly: _____		

Interpreting Your Quantitative Reasoning Score

On the ISEE, your raw score is the number of questions that you answered correctly on each section. Nothing is subtracted for the questions that you answered incorrectly.

Your raw score is then converted into a scaled score. This scaled score is then converted into a percentile score. Remember that it is the percentile score that schools are looking at. Your percentile score compares you just to other students in your grade.

Below is a chart that gives a very rough conversion between your raw score on the practice Quantitative Reasoning section and a percentile score.

PLEASE NOTE – The purpose of this chart is to let you see how the scoring works, not to give you an accurate percentile score. You will need to complete the official practice test in *What to Expect on the ISEE*, available for download from ERB at www.erblearn.org, in order to get a more accurate percentile score.

Lower Level Quantitative Reasoning

Applicants to Grade 5			
Percentile score	25th	50th	75th
Approximate raw score needed	17-18	21-22	27-28

Applicants to Grade 6			
Percentile score	25th	50th	75th
Approximate raw score needed	21-22	24-25	28-29

Reading Comprehension Answers

Correct answer	Your answer	Put a checkmark here if you answered the question correctly
1. D		
2. A		
3. B		
4. C		
5. D		
6. B		
7. D		
8. A		
9. C		
10. B		
11. A		
12. D		
13. B		
14. C		
15. D		
16. B		
17. C		
18. D		
19. D		
20. A		
21. C		
22. A		
23. B		
24. D		
25. C		
Total questions answered correctly: _____		

Interpreting Your Reading Comprehension Score

On the ISEE, your raw score is the number of questions that you answered correctly on each section. Nothing is subtracted for the questions that you answered incorrectly.

Your raw score is then converted into a scaled score. This scaled score is then converted into a percentile score. Remember that it is the percentile score that schools are looking at. Your percentile score compares you just to other students in your grade.

Below is a chart that gives a very rough conversion between your raw score on the practice Reading Comprehension section and a percentile score.

> PLEASE NOTE – The purpose of this chart is to let you see how the scoring works, not to give you an accurate percentile score. You will need to complete the official practice test in *What to Expect on the ISEE*, available for download from ERB at www.erblearn.org, in order to get a more accurate percentile score.

Lower Level Reading Comprehension

Applicants to Grade 5			
Percentile score	25th	50th	75th
Approximate raw score needed	10-11	14-15	18-19

Applicants to Grade 6			
Percentile score	25th	50th	75th
Approximate raw score needed	12-13	16-17	20-21

Mathematics Achievement Answers

Correct answer	Your answer	Put a checkmark here if you answered the question correctly
1. A		
2. C		
3. B		
4. D		
5. B		
6. C		
7. A		
8. C		
9. A		
10. D		
11. B		
12. D		
13. A		
14. C		
15. B		
16. A		
17. D		
18. C		
19. B		
20. D		
21. A		
22. C		
23. B		
24. D		
25. C		
26. D		
27. A		
28. B		
29. C		
30. C		
Total questions answered correctly: _____		

Interpreting Your Mathematics Achievement Score

On the ISEE, your raw score is the number of questions that you answered correctly on each section. Nothing is subtracted for the questions that you answered incorrectly.

Your raw score is then converted into a scaled score. This scaled score is then converted into a percentile score. Remember that it is the percentile score that schools are looking at. Your percentile score compares you just to other students in your grade.

Below is a chart that gives a very rough conversion between your raw score on the practice Mathematics Achievement section and a percentile score.

PLEASE NOTE – The purpose of this chart is to let you see how the scoring works, not to give you an accurate percentile score. You will need to complete the official practice test in *What to Expect on the ISEE*, available for download from ERB at www.erblearn.org, in order to get a more accurate percentile score.

Lower Level Mathematics Achievement

Applicants to Grade 5			
Percentile score	25th	50th	75th
Approximate raw score needed	18-19	22-23	26-27

Applicants to Grade 6			
Percentile score	25th	50th	75th
Approximate raw score needed	21-22	25-26	27-28

Looking for more instruction and practice?

Check out these other titles for the Lower Level ISEE:

Success on the Lower Level ISEE: A Complete Course

✓ Strategies to use for each section of the Lower Level ISEE

✓ Reading and vocabulary drills

✓ In-depth math content instruction with practice sets

✓ 1 full-length practice test (different from the practice tests in *The Best Unofficial Practice Tests for the Lower Level ISEE)*

30 Days to Acing the Lower Level ISEE

✓ 15 "workouts" – each a 30-minute exercise with vocabulary and practice questions for every multiple-choice section of the test

✓ Test-taking strategies for each section

Did you find *The Best Unofficial Practice Tests for the Lower Level ISEE* to be helpful? Please consider leaving a review with the merchant where you purchased the book.